Warmest personal
(mass-produced)
regards
from
Ashleigh
Brilliant

All I Want Is a Warm Bed and a Kind Word and Unlimited Power©

Even More
BRILLIANT THOUGHTS®

By Ashleigh Brilliant

Woodbridge Press/*Santa Barbara, California 93160*

1998 Printing

Published by

Woodbridge Press Publishing Company
Post Office Box 209
Santa Barbara, California 93102

Distributed simultaneously in the United States and Canada.

Printed in the United States of America.

Library of Congress Cataloging-in-Publication Data

Brilliant, Ashleigh, 1933-
  All I want is a warm bed and a kind word and unlimited power.
    Bibliography: p.
1. Epigrams, American. 2. American wit and humor, pictorial. I. Title.
PN6281.B657 1985 818'.5402 85-17973 CIP
ISBN 0-88007-155-9
ISBN 0-88007-156-7 (soft)

Dedication

This book is dedicated to the Powers That Be at the following daily newspapers, in appreciation of their exceptionally courageous and enduring support of POT-SHOTS® — and to the readers who keep twisting their arms:

The Detroit Free Press
The Seattle Times
The New Orleans Times-Picayune/States Item
The Santa Barbara News-Press
The San Diego Tribune
The Rocky Mountain News (Denver)
The Anchorage Daily News
The Oceanside (California) *Blade-Tribune*
The Greensburg (Pennsylvania) *Tribune-Review*
The Jamestown (New York) *Post-Journal*
The Traverse City (Michigan) *Record-Eagle*
The Concord (New Hampshire) *Monitor*

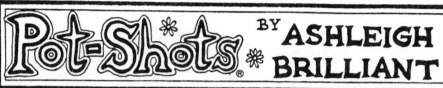

POT-SHOTS NO. 2503

ALL I WANT
IS A WARM BED
AND A KIND WORD
AND
UNLIMITED
POWER.

Ashleigh
Brilliant

Contents

GIVEN AT THE GENERAL REGISTER OFFICE,
SOMERSET HOUSE, LONDON.

1 & 2 ELIZ. 2 CH. 20

CERTIFICATE OF BIRTH

REGISTRATION DISTRICT HAMPSTEAD

1934. BIRTH in the Sub-district of Hampstead in the County of London

No.	When and where born.	Name, if any.	Sex.	Name, and surname of father.	Name, surname, and maiden surname of mother.	Occupation of father.	Signature, description, and residence of informant.	When registered.	Signature of registrar.	*Name entered after registration.
Columns:—	1	2	3	4	5	6	7	8	9	10*
419	Ninth December 1933 87 Fordwych Road	Ashleigh Ellwood	Boy	Victor Brilliant	Amelia Brilliant formerly Adler	Clerical Officer (Inland Revenue) of 47 Kendal Road Willesden	V.Brilliant Father 47 Kendal Road N.W.10	Sixteenth January 1934	A.E. Griffiths Registrar	————

*See note overleaf

CERTIFIED to be a true copy of an entry in the certified copy of a Register of Births in the District above mentioned.

Given at the GENERAL REGISTER OFFICE, SOMERSET HOUSE, LONDON, under the Seal of the said Office, the 13th day of August 195 6

BB 547893

Introduction

I'm Very Interesting To Meet You

Here we are. Or (as the case may be) here we are again: you on your side, and I on mine, of whatever strange looking glass it is that forever divides and unites reader and writer. I am Ashleigh Brilliant*. You are, for better or worse, whoever you are. We are here to initiate or resume some kind of a relationship.

If this is our first encounter, I must start by telling you what is going on, so that you can relax a little, or be more on your guard (whichever seems more appropriate). This is my fifth published collection of an apparently endless series of illustrated utterances known to the trade (and to the Trademark Office) as POT-SHOTS® or BRILLIANT THOUGHTS®, which now appear in an astounding variety of forms, including newspaper syndication, T-shirts, drinking mugs, greeting cards, posters, and calendars. I have made a bold policy of keeping them all permanently in print on postcards (the form in which they made their original commercial appearance) and offering them individually by mail order to all people everywhere regardless of age, health, or educational level. (For details on how to obtain my remarkable Catalogue, see page 165). The logistics of such an operation, with thousands of different messages now calling me their creator, are

*For proof, see Birth Certificate, preceding page.

staggering, but the game has its appealing features, one of which is that I have the privilege of making all the rules.

A Brilliant Thought® is not as simple as it may appear to be. Before it can meet your mind, it has to pass through mine, where many stern tests are imposed. One of these, I admit, is that it should appear to be simple. Others include:

1. Is it brief enough? Seventeen words is the maximum I allow myself.

2. Is it completely original, and is it sufficiently different from everything I have said before?

3. Is what it says really worth saying, and is it said in the best possible way?

4. Is it capable of being easily translated into other languages, and of being generally understood and enjoyed by the widest possible range of people?

5. Can the words be appreciated on their own, even without any illustration?

Once each Thought has passed these tests and appears in public as a child of mine, garbed with an illustration which I hope suits it well, my major concerns are (1) that it should find something useful to do in the world, and help support its father, and (2) that it should be protected from a certain form of kidnapping, all too rife in my professional neighborhood, known as copyright infringement. In pursuit of this protection, I have ventured into the legal systems of at least six countries, and every court decision, some of them involving substantial sums, has been in my favor.*

Records Shatter (Does It Matter?)

Speaking of substantial sums, this odd career as a professional epigrammatist has enabled me to claim a new world's record, as the highest paid published author (per word) in human history. According to the *Guinness Book of Records*, the previous designated champion was Ernest Hemingway, who in 1960 was offered $30,000 by *Sports Illustrated* magazine for a 2000-word article on bullfighting — a

*See particularly, *Brilliant v. WB Productions, Inc.*, U.S. District Court, Los Angeles, Civil Action #CV79-1893-WMB, judgment entered October 22, 1979. $18,000 awarded and collected.

rate of $15 per word. But on December 30, 1981, that same magazine offered me $5,000 simply for the right to use 12 of my words in a television commercial — a rate of $416.66 per word. What dozen words could possibly be so valuable? It was Brilliant Thought® No. 433, which happens also be the title of my first book: I MAY NOT BE TOTALLY PERFECT, BUT PARTS OF ME ARE EXCELLENT.© And if you don't find that instance sufficiently impressive from a literary point of view (since, after all, *Sports Illustrated* is not preeminent as an authority on epigrams), allow me then to cite the case of the Hallmark Card Company of Kansas City, Missouri, which is beyond question the world's largest buyer and seller of such material. In 1982, that august entity paid me $15,000 just as an advance on royalties for the rights to use four of my works, totalling 44 words, on their cards — a rate of $340.91 per word.

The Power and the Glory

I care not who writes my country's laws,
But let me write its Brilliant Thoughts.®

But even Kansas City, it must be confessed, is not the height of my ambition. Conscious of my pioneering role in creating a totally new form of creative expression, I have set my sights upon securing the most elevated forms of recognition and status for my craft, and for my crafty self as its progenitor. Such honors can appear in many different guises, some of them quite surprising. In 1979, for example, I was accorded the tasteful distinction of having a new salad named after me (the Ashleigh Brilliant Turkey Salad, Earthling Bookstore/Tea Room, Santa Barbara). And there was the time a U.S. Federal Agent, purely because he enjoyed my work, used the awesome power of his well-known Bureau of Investigation to help me track down an elusive distributor of "motto" cards, some of which had illicitly taken on an uncanny resemblance to Pot-Shots.® And once (as I thought happened only in the movies) a city policeman who was about to give me a traffic ticket actually changed his mind upon discovering my identity, and instead took out his own wallet to show me the Pot-Shots® he always carried in it, clipped from his local paper.

POT-SHOTS NO. 3343.

IF I HAD MORE SKILL IN WHAT I'M ATTEMPTING

Ashleigh Brilliant

I WOULDN'T NEED SO MUCH COURAGE.

Then there have been those serendipitous moments of finding my works on sale in completely unexpected places. On one occasion, when nothing could have been further from my thoughts, I suddenly came upon a rack of them (on postcards) at the top of Victoria Peak in Hong Kong. Another time, I found an impressive display of my books on the counter of a small bookstore in Darwin, in the remote Northern Territory of Australia, an area which to me until then had been a virtual Ultima Thule, but which I now realized, from this evidence alone, is a civilized and highly cultured community.

But, as a writer of full-length works which are only too easily dismissed as mere "one-liners," simply because they never exceed seventeen words, I deem no glory more glittering than to be celebrated at gatherings of "real" authors, such as the prestigious annual Santa Barbara Writers Conference, where as a featured speaker I have found myself sharing the limelight with literary luminaries whose works invariably run to many thousands of words. As you might expect, I generally utilize these opportunities of addressing my fellow writers by making lengthy pleas on behalf of brevity.

Another way of measuring my success would, I suppose, be in terms of the lengths to which any devoted fan might go in order to have personal contact with me. While there may have been other less well-documented cases, it is on record that one Pot-Shots® enthusiast, Mr. John Mohler, at the age of 68, travelled alone from his home in Walnut Creek, California, to Sonoma State University in Rohnert Park, California, a distance of some 40 miles (64.372 km.), for the sole purpose of seeing me perform at the final meeting of a six-week summer session course in Recent Social History which I was teaching there. Hoping to attract a huge throng, I had, in the official description, promised that the course would dwell "with particular fondness upon heroes, scandals, cults, crazes, disasters, songs, jokes, hoaxes, and other culturally illuminating phenomena." Mr. Mohler's presence on that memorable occasion (July 27, 1978) brought the attendance to a record total of seven (including another fervent fan, my wife, Dorothy).* It is also true (though I still find it hard to

*The shadow of her 1968 smile is on Pot-Shot® No. 3461 in Chapter XII.

believe) that an entire church congregation in Dallas, Texas, once had me travel to that city as their guest simply as a "present" for their minister who was celebrating his fourth anniversary in that office and who was so fond of my work that he and his wife had an enlarged Brilliant Thought® hung on the wall above their bed. (Pot Shot® No. 62: WE OUGHT TO BE MORE CAREFUL — OUR LOVE COULD DRAG ON FOR YEARS AND YEARS.)

For sheer Brilliant FANtasy, however, the cake is surely taken by Mr. Herbert Murrie, the President of California Dreamers, a soaringly successful greeting-card company which is actually located in Chicago. In 1984, this admirable admirer not only conceived the spectacular idea of bringing out a whole new card line of Brilliant Thoughts,® but had me wafted from half a continent away, just so that I might sign the contract in his beaming presence. To fill my own cup of joy to overflowing, he also agreed that each of the new cards (on which his company would be using only my words, combined with their own art) would, in a wild departure from industry practice, have my name as author printed immediately following the words, in a fashion usually reserved for such widely quoted (but unpaid) eminences as William Shakespeare and Henry David Thoreau.

All of this could go to my head, were it not for my keen awareness of the vain and transitory nature of fame, combined with an almost indecent lust for much more of it than I am ever likely to get (at least from my contemporaries — I cannot speak for Posterity, not having been authorized to do so). Indeed, I have probably made it much harder for myself ever to secure a Pulitzer or Nobel Prize by publicly and repeatedly declaring that I am specifically in the market for them. But this is really part of my plan, since only by making my life's objective sufficiently difficult can I be sure that I won't attain it too soon, and then be faced with the onerous task of choosing another life's objective.

It should be noted, however, that my first book actually was nominated for a Pulitzer Prize (an achievement within reach of any published author capable of filling in the required nomination form — but I modestly requested my publisher to do it on my behalf). And an actual recipient of that award (for General Nonfiction, 1980) has in a later work not only quoted seven of my Thoughts and listed all my books in his bibliography, but also, apparently in anticipation of greater things to come, taken it upon himself to award me the "Nobaloney Prize for Aphoristic Eloquence." (Douglas R. Hofstadter, *Metamagical Themas: Questing for the Essence of Mind and Pattern*. New York: Basic Books, 1985, pp. 47, 732, 803.)*

Life Stages

If I ever do come to be ranked with the likes of Ernest Hemingway on any other level than the size of our respective paychecks, certain questions beloved of scholars are bound to come up, which, to round off this introductory section, I might as well attempt to answer here:

1. What Were the Major Influences on His Work?

Sir Isaac Newton modestly claimed to have "stood on the shoulders of giants" — but for me the only shoulders available were those of my parents. My mother, Amelia Brilliant, one of the world's most prolific communicators, deserves credit as the first person to find any utility in my own talents, encouraging me from an early age to make greeting cards for our family. My father, Victor Brilliant (1898-1972), a British career civil servant, had a great love of jokes and word-play, but was so surprised when, towards the end of his life, I started proving that his only son could make a living at such pursuits, that he rather uncharacteristically began to call me a "genius."

For general inspiration, I probably also owe a profound debt to two classes of anonymous writers whose productions pervade our society: (1) the masterly wordsmiths of Advertising (who must envy me because my work has nothing to sell but itself) and (2) the industrious perpetrators of Graffiti, to whose sometimes very imaginative works I have so often been exposed, particularly on the walls of small rooms providing considerable privacy both to the original inscriber and to the subsequent reader and student.

*For other Brilliant literary references, see Bibliography, p. 166.

POT-SHOTS NO. 3444.

Pot-Shots

BY ASHLEIGH BRILLIANT

THE SECRET OF
SELLING
YOURSELF

IS
TO HAVE
A PRODUCT
YOU TRULY
BELIEVE IN.

Ashleigh Brilliant

2. When Did He First Become Fully Cognizant of His Own Abilities?

My peculiar power with brief verbal expressions was not revealed to me until 1964, in Berkeley, California, when, at the age of 30, to celebrate my sense of liberation after securing my Ph.D. in History, for the first time in my life I began publicly displaying some of my paintings and drawings, and attempting to sell them. These particular works were of a generally abstract or surrealistic nature, but I was fascinated to discover that people would sometimes buy one, not primarily because of the "picture," but because they liked the few words I had written inconspicuously at the bottom as a title. This led me to theorize that a "title" could be a work in itself, and to begin writing lists of titles for pictures which never materialized. After a purely verbal period, during which I used to recite these lines as poems, and in fact called them "Unpoemed Titles," the wheel came full circle when I decided to add illustrations, and in 1967 began publishing them as postcards.

3. What Dramatic Incidents Highlighted His Career?

My career as a postcard-prophet might not, however, have gone very far had it not been for a piece of sensational luck. In September, 1968, the Bohn Rex-Rotary duplicating equipment company informed me that my name had been selected from thousands entered in a nationwide "lucky drawing" conducted by their firm, and I became the owner of one of their electronic stencil-cutters, then priced at a (for me) impossible $1,400. It was this feat which enabled me to go into business in San Francisco as an independent printer of my own postcards, with all the earth-shaking consequences of that move.

By earth-shaking contrast, the most destructive force ever unleashed against my Thoughts was that of a completely uncalled-for major earthquake (5.1 on the Richter scale), which struck Santa Barbara (to which I had moved in 1973) on August 13, 1978, and malevolently toppled several of my shelves with their thousands of cards. No lives or ideas were lost, however, and this anti-intellectual disaster spent most of its efforts at our local University, where some 281,000 books in the library all suddenly found themselves in need of reshelving, and total damage costs reached $5.5 million.

My most dramatic copyright confrontation occurred in London in 1972. An excessively enterprising shopkeeper, seeing how well my cards were selling in his establishment, had the temerity to bring out a competing line of his own, using all my same words but substituting other pictures, apparently in the false belief that this would make such wholesale theft "legal." It cost me some trouble to provide him with a speedy education on that point, but the upshot was that, in addition to financial penalties, the judge ordered that all 48,000 of the infringing cards should be delivered to me for immediate destruction.

I had never before been required to DESTROY a large number of postcards, and the task was not as easy as you might think, especially as I was in the middle of a large city where burning of waste was not permitted and I still had to make sure that none of the offending material could ever possibly be salvaged to reappear upon the market. My eventual solution was found at a demolition site. After laboriously carrying all the boxes of cards there and emptying them into a huge dumpster, I borrowed a hose and soaked them with water, then paid a workman to cover them with rubble and dirt as I watched. This was done only after I had ascertained that all debris from that location was to be hauled to the river, placed on barges, and dumped far at sea. (But I took that part on faith, and did not follow my abused and soggy words on their sad final voyage.)

But if you are looking for real drama in my life, the last word surely belongs to an actual dramatic work, called *Begetting,* which I wrote in 1980, and in 1985 somehow induced a brave group of local players to give its premier production in my own community. Like many a playwright's first fruits, it was largely autobiographical, and, although the event was not widely publicized, I could not help feeling that the response of the critics would be as much a statement about my life as about my play.

The response indicated a certain lack of concern. Only one critic actually came — and even he began his review by admitting that he had missed much of the first act through arriving late and being unable to find a way in. (This did indeed seem darkly significant. How many other people have been unsuccessfully trying to find their way into my life?) He went on to praise several of the performers, but seemed to have had difficulties with the story, and, as if speaking for the hero, protested that, if there was a moral, it had escaped him. It is not clear whether he had ever come across Brilliant Thought® No. 144: "MY LIFE HAS A MARVELLOUS CAST, BUT I CAN'T FIGURE OUT THE PLOT." But such experiences as this may help to explain why, far from having achieved unlimited power, I am still looking for a warm bed and a kind word.

POT-SHOTS NO. 3373.   Ashleigh Brilliant

THERE WILL BE
A SLIGHT DELAY,
WHILE I TRY
TO REMEMBER
WHY
I WAS BORN.

© ASHLEIGH BRILLIANT 1985.

I. I Go Ego

In this life, whatever it is, you have to start from wherever you are. Where you are, for better or worse, is somewhere inside a human being. You know the location is only temporary, but you've been there as long as you can remember, and can't really even imagine what it's like to be anywhere else. Still, you're not always comfortable, and are forced to make increasingly frequent repairs and adjustments, simply to keep the place habitable.

When not thus preoccupied, you try, like any other prisoner, to fill the time by exploring the area of your confinement. It is called a "self." It has some dark corners, and there are many things about it which you don't understand. But one thing is clear beyond all doubt: you are utterly alone in it.

There is only one door, which seems so mysterious and frightening that you tend to stay far away from it. But here and there you find many small windows, through which you can peer and even reach — and thus you become aware of other captives imprisoned in other selves.

In time, you discover that an elaborate communication system exists. Brief messages such as mine are popular because they pass easily through the cracks in the walls. And, as might be expected, the first thoughts exchanged (like those in this opening section) often deal with this strange condition of selfhood in which we solitary senders are doomed to spend our days.

I HAVE
DECIDED
TO DEVOTE
MY ENTIRE
CAREER
TO
LOOKING FOR
A CAREER.

POT-SHOTS NO. 3362.

©ASHLEIGH BRILLIANT 1985.

POT-SHOTS NO. 3188.

MY LIFE
WOULD BE
A MORE
SATISFYING
DRAMA,
IF
APPROPRIATE
MUSIC
WERE ALWAYS
PLAYING
IN THE
BACKGROUND.

©ASHLEIGH BRILLIANT 1985.

©ASHLEIGH BRILLIANT 1985.

POT-SHOTS NO. 3202.

HOW DO
I EVER
FIND
THE TIME
TO
ACCOMPLISH
SO LITTLE
AND SUFFER
SO MUCH?

I SEEM TO HAVE A NATURAL GIFT

FOR PLAYING A GAME

WHICH UNFORTUNATELY HASN'T YET BEEN INVENTED.

Ashleigh Brilliant

It's only because I want everything I do to be perfect that I never actually do anything.

Ashleigh Brilliant

Why is it
that,
whenever
I have
an appointment
with myself,
I'm always
late?

I HAVE WASTED
MUCH TIME ON
VAIN REGRETS ~

IN FACT,
THAT'S ONE OF
MY BIGGEST
REGRETS.

Where
I come from
and where
I belong
are
not necessarily
the same
place.

POT-SHOTS NO. 3328.

COPING WITH DIFFICULT PEOPLE IS ALWAYS A PROBLEM,

Ashleigh Brilliant

PARTICULARLY
IF THE
DIFFICULT
PERSON
HAPPENS TO BE
ONESELF.

POT-SHOTS NO. 3313.

I MARCH TO A DIFFERENT DRUMMER,

Ashleigh Brilliant

WHOSE LOCATION,
IDENTITY,
AND
MUSICAL TRAINING
HAVEN'T YET
BEEN ESTABLISHED.

POT-SHOTS NO.3335.

I NEED MORE PROOF,

BEFORE
I CAN BE
ABSOLUTELY
CERTAIN
THAT
I DO NOT
EXIST.

Ashleigh Brilliant

HOW CAN I BE SURE I'VE SUCCEEDED,

Ashleigh
Brilliant

IF I CAN'T REMEMBER WHAT I WAS TRYING TO DO?

ALL MIGHT BE WELL,

IF THIS WERE ANOTHER PLACE AT ANOTHER TIME,

Ashleigh
Brilliant

AND I WERE ANOTHER PERSON.

POT-SHOTS NO. 3432.

Ashleigh
Brilliant

I'M SURE MY EFFORTS DESERVE MY GOALS,

BUT SOMETIMES WONDER IF MY GOALS ARE WORTH MY EFFORTS.

POT-SHOTS NO. 3408.

Somehow, I have to believe that I'm worth all the aggravation I cause myself.

Ashleigh
Brilliant

I KNEW I WOULDN'T REACH PERFECTION OVERNIGHT,

BUT WHY AREN'T I ANY CLOSER THAN I AM?

© ASHLEIGH BRILLIANT 1985.

Ashleigh Brilliant

© ASHLEIGH BRILLIANT 1985.

POT-SHOTS NO. 3356.

WHAT'S THE GOOD OF BEING GREEDY,

Ashleigh Brilliant

IF NOTHING I WANT IS AVAILABLE?

POT-SHOTS NO. 3489.

THE CLUB CALLED EARTH

OFFERS VERY SPECIAL FACILITIES,—

Ashleigh Brilliant

AND I'VE BEEN GIVEN A LIFETIME MEMBERSHIP!

© ASHLEIGH BRILLIANT 1985.

POT-SHOTS NO. 3513.

Ashleigh Brilliant

I'VE BEEN HERE IN THE MIDDLE FOR SO LONG

THAT I'VE FORGOTTEN WHAT IT'S THE MIDDLE OF.

POT-SHOTS NO. 3308.

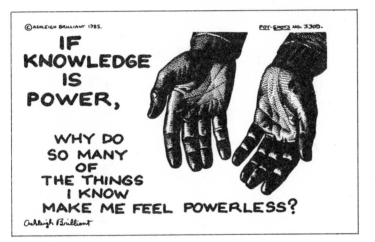

IF KNOWLEDGE IS POWER,

WHY DO SO MANY OF THE THINGS I KNOW MAKE ME FEEL POWERLESS?

Ashleigh Brilliant

POT-SHOTS NO. 3227.

Ashleigh Brilliant

IT'S NO USE HAVING A GOOD MEMORY,

UNLESS YOU HAVE SOMETHING GOOD TO REMEMBER.

I Go Ego 29

POT-SHOTS NO. 3443.

I WISH
I COULD GET
A MIRROR
WITH
A BETTER
VIEW.

©ASHLEIGH BRILLIANT 1985.

Ashleigh Brilliant

©ASHLEIGH BRILLIANT 1985.

POT-SHOTS NO. 3300.

ALL I ASK

Ashleigh Brilliant

IS THAT
I NEVER
FEEL LIKE
MYSELF
AGAIN.

©ASHLEIGH BRILLIANT 1985.

POT-SHOTS NO. 3474.

Ashleigh Brilliant

IF
ANYTHING
GOES WRONG
WITH MY
LIFE,

WHOM
SHOULD
I HOLD
RESPONSIBLE
?

Ashleigh
Brilliant

I TOO COULD BE SUCCESSFUL,

IF I HAD MONEY, TALENT, LUCK, CHARM, CONFIDENCE, AND PLENTY OF HELP.

©ASHLEIGH BRILLIANT 1985.

Ashleigh Brilliant

NO ANNOUNCEMENT OF MY DEATH CAN BE CONSIDERED OFFICIAL,

UNLESS I MAKE IT IN PERSON.

©ASHLEIGH BRILLIANT 1985.

I Go Ego 31

Pot-Shots BY **ASHLEIGH BRILLIANT**

POT-SHOTS NO. 3195.

Ashleigh Brilliant

© ASHLEIGH BRILLIANT 1985

PLEASE KEEP
YOUR MIND
OPEN,

UNTIL
I CAN GET
A LITTLE MORE
OF MY
ARGUMENT
INTO IT.

II. An Eye for a You

One person may be quite enough to occupy a single self; but for any meaningful dialogue to take place, the existence of Someone Else is a basic requirement. That condition being fulfilled, there is almost no limit to the complex linking edifices which can in time be erected.

But, just as the greatest bridges are often begun by throwing a single strand over the chasm, so the most involved relationships can at times depend upon a mere thread of words strung from mind to mind. As a specialist in this kind of delicate engineering, I must assemble my words and wind them around each other with exquisite care, never having more than seventeen of them available to stretch all the way from a me to a you.

The consequences of inferior workmanship in this craft can be truly catastrophic. As the result of a botched sequence of words, whole friendships have been known to collapse, and even mighty marriages to fall asunder. When well-made, however, and of course when correctly used, a good person-to-person message can be as dazzling in its effect as a string of bright lights dipping across the lonely darkness.

EVEN IF I'M SOMETIMES UNFAITHFUL,

YOU'LL
ALWAYS BE
THE PERSON
I WANT TO BE
UNFAITHFUL TO.

Ashleigh Brilliant

HOW WOULD YOU RATE ME,

ON A SCALE OF
WONDERFUL
TO
MARVELOUS?

Ashleigh Brilliant

AS LONG AS
I HAVE YOU,
THERE'S JUST
ONE OTHER THING
I'LL ALWAYS
NEED:~

POT-SHOTS NO. 3197.
Ashleigh Brilliant
© ASHLEIGH BRILLIANT 1985.

TREMENDOUS
SELF-CONTROL.

POT-SHOTS NO. 3387.

I KNEW
SOMETHING
WAS WRONG
THE MOMENT
YOU BIT
MY NOSE.

©ASHLEIGH BRILLIANT 1985.
Ashleigh Brilliant

An Eye for a You 35

TELESCOPES
AND MICROSCOPES
ARE WONDERFUL,

BUT THE BEST
OPTICAL INSTRUMENTS
FOR
SEEING ME
ARE STILL
YOUR
EYES.

© ASHLEIGH BRILLIANT 1985.

© ASHLEIGH BRILLIANT 1985.

IF YOU
DON'T
KNOW
WHAT
YOU'RE
LOOKING
FOR,

MY PLACE
IS A GOOD PLACE
TO START LOOKING.

© ASHLEIGH BRILLIANT 1985.

WOULD
YOU
RATHER BE
WHERE
YOU
OUGHT
TO BE,
OR
WITH ME?

YOU HAVE YOUR PROBLEMS,

AND I HAVE YOURS.

POT-SHOTS NO. 3376

Ashleigh Brilliant   POT-SHOTS NO. 3393.

NOT ENOUGH PROGRESS IS BEING MADE

by you towards me.

POT-SHOTS NO. 3383.

THERE'S NO ROOM IN THIS ARGUMENT FOR BOTH OF US,

UNLESS YOU MOVE OVER A LITTLE.

Ashleigh Brilliant

POT-SHOTS NO. 3423.

Ashleigh Brilliant

Did you receive all the good wishes I sent you?

If so, did they have any effect?

©ASHLEIGH BRILLIANT 1985.

POT-SHOTS NO. 3442.

Ashleigh Brilliant

WHY ARE YOU BOMBARDING ME

WITH YOUR SILENCE?

©ASHLEIGH BRILLIANT 1985.

©ASHLEIGH BRILLIANT 1985.

POT-SHOTS NO. 3437.

IT'S GOOD TO KNOW I CAN ALWAYS DEPEND ON YOUR HALF-HEARTED SUPPORT.

Ashleigh Brilliant

© ASHLEIGH BRILLIANT 1985.

POT-SHOTS NO. 3447.

IN THE INTEREST OF BETTER HUMAN RELATIONS

SHOULD WE SEE MORE OF EACH OTHER, OR LESS?

Ashleigh Brilliant

© ASHLEIGH BRILLIANT 1985.

POT-SHOTS NO. 3458.

Ashleigh Brilliant

ONE THING THAT WILL NEVER CHANGE IS THE NEED OF PEOPLE LIKE ME FOR PEOPLE LIKE YOU.

© ASHLEIGH BRILLIANT 1985.

POT-SHOTS NO. 3460.

Ashleigh Brilliant

IF YOU'RE INTERESTED IN ESTABLISHING A FRIENDSHIP,

LET'S BEGIN THE NEGOTIATIONS.

An Eye for a You 39

Would you rather be in my mood, or have me come into yours?

©ASHLEIGH BRILLIANT 1985.

Ashleigh Brilliant

I DIDN'T KNOW PEOPLE LIKE YOU WERE STILL BEING PRODUCED.

©ASHLEIGH BRILLIANT 1985.

Ashleigh Brilliant

GET BETTER!

THERE'S NOTHING BETTER THAN A BETTER YOU.

Ashleigh Brilliant

©ASHLEIGH BRILLIANT 1985.

© ASHLEIGH BRILLIANT 1985

POT-SHOTS NO. 3314.

I ALWAYS WIN — YOU ALWAYS LOSE —

Ashleigh Brilliant

WHAT COULD BE FAIRER THAN THAT?

POT-SHOTS NO. 3192.

Ashleigh Brilliant

© ASHLEIGH BRILLIANT 1985.

HUMAN NATURE WILL EVENTUALLY REACH PERFECTION ~

IN THE MEANTIME, LET'S TRY TO FORGIVE OURSELVES AND EACH OTHER.

POT-SHOTS NO. 3503.

I DON'T NEED THE KIND OF PROBLEMS YOU GIVE ME ~

THEY'RE A PURE LUXURY.

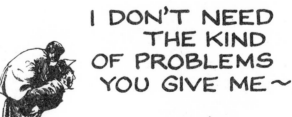

© ASHLEIGH BRILLIANT 1985.

Ashleigh Brilliant

Ashleigh Brilliant

MY LIFE IS VERY DELICATELY BALANCED:

PLEASE
DON'T
MAKE
ANY
SUDDEN
MOVEMENTS.

WHY MUST I SPEND SO MUCH OF MY LIFE

CONVINCING
YOU
OF
WHAT'S
SO
OBVIOUS
TO ME?

Ashleigh
Brilliant

HOW MUCH MUST I CHANGE TO SATISFY YOU? ~

Ashleigh
Brilliant

AND
WOULD ANYTHING
BE LEFT
OF THE
ORIGINAL ME?

POT-SHOTS NO. 3271.

THERE'S A PRICE
FOR HUMILIATING ME,
AND, IF YOU DON'T PAY IT, I'LL FEEL EVEN MORE HUMILIATED.

POT-SHOTS NO. 3384.

I'M NOT FORGIVING BY NATURE,
BUT, FORTUNATELY FOR SOME PEOPLE, I'M VERY FORGETFUL.

POT-SHOTS NO. 3417.

I LIKE THE OLD ME,
BUT I'D LOVE TO HAVE A NEW YOU.

An Eye for a You 43

POT-SHOTS NO. 3472.

I KEEP FINDING
STRANGE LITTLE
SIGNS THAT
I MAY NOT BE
THE ONLY
PERSON
IN THE
WORLD.

Ashleigh Brilliant

III. Other Wise

Regardless of the calendar date, allow me to wish you a happy Others Day, celebrating, as we are forced to do every day, the existence of those peculiarly distinguished beings called Others, whom we are taught from infancy always deserve our special consideration. For reasons hard to fathom, and contrary to all basic instincts, they are enshrined in our Golden Rule, and have become the super-heroes of our entire moral code. Verily, it seems their entire purpose in life is nothing more significant than to be the eternal beneficiaries of our unselfishness.

No doubt because of this very lenient policy, the world is chock-full of them. They clutter the streets, the schools, the shops. Their cars fill all the parking places. Their trivial conversations monopolize the telephone booths. Often not even in our homes are we safe from their constant need to be taken into account, soothed, and treated as if they were really more important than we are.

No Brilliant thinker can entirely avoid coming to grips with this widespread problem. The following messages, as will be seen, accept the fact of Otherhood with a certain weary resignation, if only because there seems to be no longer any reasonable hope of stamping it out.

POT-SHOTS NO. 3183.

WHY DO I GET SO LITTLE THANKS FOR THE MANY THINGS I DO THAT NOBODY WANTS DONE?

Ashleigh Brilliant

POT-SHOTS NO. 3212.

THERE MUST BE SOMETHING IN THE AIR

THAT MAKES ME WANT TO KEEP BREATHING IT.

Ashleigh Brilliant

POT-SHOTS NO. 3228.

I LIKE TO STUDY TOURISTS IN THEIR NATIVE HABITAT.

Ashleigh Brilliant

POT-SHOTS NO. 3174.

Ashleigh Brilliant

PLEASE DON'T JUDGE ME

BY WHAT I SAY
OR DO
OR THINK

OR REALLY AM.

POT-SHOTS NO. 3225

Ashleigh Brilliant

ALL I NEED FOR TOTAL CONTROL

IS FOR EVERYBODY ELSE TO BE TOTALLY SUBMISSIVE.

Other Wise 47

I AM A PERSON OF MYSTERY~

THE MYSTERY IS WHY I TELL EVERYBODY SO MUCH ABOUT MYSELF.

SOME PEOPLE OWE ME AN APOLOGY

FOR KNOWING SO MUCH MORE THAN I DO.

IT'S SURPRISING HOW MANY PEOPLE SEEM TO THINK THEY HAVE A RIGHT TO GIVE ME TROUBLE.

ONE OF THE THINGS
I MOST
ENJOY
RECEIVING

IS
OBEDIENCE.

POT-SHOTS NO. 3218

IF ONLY
IT WERE
ALWAYS
MY PATRIOTIC
DUTY

TO HAVE
UNLIMITED
PLEASURE.

POT-SHOTS NO. 3502.

I hope
I live
long enough
to be
forgiven
for
some things
I haven't
even done yet.

SOMETIMES
I WONDER

IF
THE WORLD
REALLY
HAS
MY BEST
INTERESTS
AT HEART.

© ASHLEIGH BRILLIANT 1985.

THE
COUNTRYSIDE
NEVER
CLOSES.

© ASHLEIGH BRILLIANT 1985.

Ashleigh Brilliant

WHY DO
SO MANY
PEOPLE
FIND IT
SO EASY
TO
CONTROL
THEIR
CRAVING
FOR ME?

© ASHLEIGH BRILLIANT 1985.

POT-SHOTS NO. 3266.

WHY
ARE
THERE
SO MANY
PEOPLE
I'D RATHER
SEE
IN MY MEMORY
THAN ON
MY DOORSTEP?

Ashleigh Brilliant

Ashleigh Brilliant

POT-SHOTS NO. 3287.

WHICH SIDE
OF MY BRAIN

CONTROLS
INTERNATIONAL
EVENTS?

POT-SHOTS NO. 3345.

Ashleigh Brilliant

I HOPE I NEVER BECOME SO WIDELY LOVED AND RESPECTED

THAT SOMEBODY SOMEWHERE

WANTS TO KILL ME.

POT-SHOTS NO. 3377.

Ashleigh Brilliant

THE LESS ANYBODY WANTS YOU,

THE LESS VALUABLE YOU BECOME,

UNLESS YOU REALLY WANT YOURSELF.

POT-SHOTS NO. 3448.

THE WORLD HAS A RIGHT TO DISAGREE WITH ME,

BUT OUGHT TO GIVE MY ARGUMENTS MORE CONSIDERATION.

Ashleigh Brilliant

THE ONLY WAY
TO BE SURE
OF SURVIVING

IS
NEVER TO
DO ANYTHING
FOR THE
LAST TIME.

Ashleigh Brilliant

©ASHLEIGH
BRILLIANT
1985

©ASHLEIGH BRILLIANT 1985.

POT-SHOTS NO. 3307.

WHY
SHOULD I
ASK FOR
HELP,

WHEN,
IN A
PERFECT
WORLD,
IT WOULD COME
WITHOUT
MY ASKING?

Ashleigh Brilliant

©ASHLEIGH BRILLIANT 1985.

POT-SHOTS NO. 3350.
Ashleigh Brilliant

I TRY TO SEE
ALL SIDES
OF THE
QUESTION

—perhaps
that's why
my eyes
get so tired.

Other Wise 53

POT-SHOTS NO. 3320.

I WANT EVERYONE TO BE HAPPY~

AT LEAST HAPPY ENOUGH SO THAT NOBODY COMES BOTHERING ME.

Ashleigh Brilliant

POT-SHOTS NO. 3430.

I LIKE WHO I AM,

AND AM PUZZLED TO FIND THAT NOT EVERYBODY SHARES THIS OPINION.

Ashleigh Brilliant

Ashleigh Brilliant

POT-SHOTS NO. 3419.

MY CAT KNOWS THE MEANING OF LIFE,

BUT HAS NO INTEREST IN SHARING THE SECRET.

POT-SHOTS NO. 3468.

Ashleigh Brilliant

IT'S NO GOOD BEING FAMOUS,

UNLESS THE PEOPLE YOU KNOW KNOW HOW FAMOUS YOU ARE.

POT-SHOTS NO. 3427

IF I CAN'T
BE ANGRY
BECAUSE
I'M INFERIOR,
WHAT CAN I
BE ANGRY ABOUT?

Ashleigh Brilliant

POT-SHOTS NO. 3200.

AT WHAT POINT
IN MY STRUGGLE
WITH NATURE
WILL NATURE
FINALLY
GIVE UP?

Ashleigh Brilliant

POT-SHOTS NO. 3243.

I ALWAYS KNOW WHEN I'M CONSCIOUS

BUT, FOR SOME STRANGE REASON, I NEVER KNOW WHEN I'M UNCONSCIOUS.

© ASHLEIGH BRILLIANT 1985.

IV. Who's Minding the Body?

Where would most of us be without our Bodies and Minds? One thing, at least, is certain: we would not be in this chapter, of which those intriguing entities are the principal subject.

Being both mental and physical at the same time, twenty-four hours a day in all kinds of weather, is a demanding task which I personally feel deserves far more credit than you or I are ever likely to receive. Particularly meritorious is our capacity to keep the Body nicely "idling" or "turning over" while the Mind is engaged in performing those elegant nocturnal acrobatics called dreams.

For top performance, of course, the most important requirement is that rare condition known as Perfect Health, characterized by a total absence of symptoms, and hardly even referred to in the medical literature. At the opposite end of the spectrum there is a totally inactive state which (for lack of a better term) is usually described as being "dead."

Between these two extremes, our strange twosome of Mind and Body shuffles uncertainly along from day to day, sometimes very oddly paired, and occasionally not even on speaking terms, but always chained together under an indeterminate sentence called "Life."

POT-SHOTS NO. 3512.

Ashleigh Brilliant

IT CAN TAKE A SURPRISINGLY LONG TIME

TO GET
FROM
ONE PART
OF MY MIND
TO ANOTHER.

POT-SHOTS NO. 3366.

Ashleigh Brilliant

TAKE HEART!

MANY
GREAT THINGS
HAVE
BEEN DONE
BY
PEOPLE
IN POOR
MENTAL
HEALTH.

POT-SHOTS NO. 3511.

Ashleigh Brilliant

QUICK!
CALL
A
WITCH-DOCTOR:

MY WITCH
IS SICK!

Ashleigh Brilliant POT-SHOTS NO. 3494.

IF YOU CAN HEAR SOMEONE SNORING,

AT LEAST YOU KNOW YOU'RE NOT ALONE IN THE UNIVERSE.

POT-SHOTS NO. 3476.

I DON'T LIKE BEING WOKEN UP ~

I CONSIDER IT AN INTRUSION ON MY PRIVACY.

POT-SHOTS NO. 3425.

Ashleigh Brilliant

IT'S POSSIBLE TO FEEL HEALTHY AT ANY AGE,

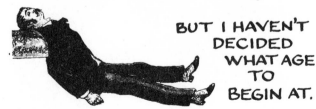

BUT I HAVEN'T DECIDED WHAT AGE TO BEGIN AT.

Who's Minding the Body?

POT-SHOTS NO. 3500.

MY DREAMS ARE NOT DEAD ~

Ashleigh Brilliant

THEY'RE ONLY SLEEPING.

POT-SHOTS NO. 3304.

THERE'S NOTHING ON MY MIND

THAT COULDN'T BE EXPRESSED BY A LONG INSANE OUTBURST OF HYSTERICAL RAGE.

Ashleigh Brilliant

Ashleigh Brilliant   POT-SHOTS NO. 3426.

I HATE ARGUMENTS,

PARTICULARLY ARGUMENTS BETWEEN THE WATCH ON MY WRIST AND THE CLOCK IN MY BODY.

©ASHLEIGH BRILLIANT 1985.

POT-SHOTS NO. 3324.

Ashleigh Brilliant

THE MORE LIKELY CAUSES OF DEATH I AVOID,

THE MORE CHANCE I'LL DIE IN SOME UNLIKELY WAY.

©ASHLEIGH BRILLIANT 1985.

©ASHLEIGH BRILLIANT 1985.

POT-SHOTS NO. 3407.

Ashleigh Brilliant

YOUR OWN COMMON SENSE SHOULD TELL YOU

THAT COMMON SENSE ALONE IS NOT ENOUGH.

POT-SHOTS NO. 3305.

WHAT IS THE BEST LUBRICANT

FOR
A LIFE
THAT'S
NOT RUNNING
VERY SMOOTHLY?

© ASHLEIGH BRILLIANT 1985.

© ASHLEIGH BRILLIANT 1985.

POT-SHOTS NO. 3284.

HOW CAN I WAKE YOU UP,

Ashleigh Brilliant

WITHOUT
SHATTERING
YOUR
DREAMS?

Ashleigh Brilliant

POT-SHOTS NO. 3283.

MY MIND IS HOLDING MY BODY HOSTAGE ~

AND
DEMANDING
SAFE-CONDUCT
OUT OF
THE WORLD.

© ASHLEIGH BRILLIANT 1985.

BY USING YOUR INTELLIGENCE,

YOU CAN
SOMETIMES
MAKE
YOUR PROBLEMS
TWICE AS COMPLICATED.

Ashleigh Brilliant

I HOPE YOUR RECURRING DREAMS

ARE
THE KIND
YOU LIKE
TO GO BACK TO.

HOLD YOUR HEAD HIGH!

— GOOD
POSTURE
IS SOMETHING
TO BE PROUD OF.

Who's Minding the Body? 63

POT-SHOTS NO. 3250.

WHY IS IT
THAT MY
WORST
DREAMS

ARE THOSE
WHICH
MOST CLOSELY
RESEMBLE
REAL
LIFE?

© ASHLEIGH BRILLIANT 1985

© ASHLEIGH BRILLIANT 1985.

POT-SHOTS NO. 3178.

NONE OF
MY WOUNDS

REQUIRE
MORE TENDER,
LOVING,
TREATMENT

THAN THOSE
I'VE INFLICTED
ON MYSELF.

Ashleigh Brilliant

© ASHLEIGH BRILLIANT 1985.

POT-SHOTS NO. 3337.

Ashleigh
Brilliant

Why does
merely attempting
to understand
Reality
so often
seem to
lead to
going
insane?

MY MIND
CONTAINS
MANY
GOOD IDEAS,

BUT
IT'S NOT
ALWAYS
EASY TO
SQUEEZE
ONE OUT.

© ASHLEIGH BRILLIANT 1985

POT-SHOTS NO. 3171 © ASHLEIGH BRILLIANT 1985

AS LONG AS
YOU HAVE
YOUR FEET
ON THE
GROUND,

YOUR HEAD IS
PERFECTLY SAFE
IN THE
CLOUDS.

POT-SHOTS NO. 3176. © ASHLEIGH BRILLIANT 1985.

GOOD NEWS,
IF YOU
ENJOY LIVING:

ALMOST EVERYBODY
ALIVE TODAY
CAN REASONABLY
EXPECT TO BE
ALIVE TOMORROW!

THE MAIN REQUIREMENT FOR DOING EVERYTHING YOU WANT TO DO

IS: STAYING ALIVE.

Ashleigh Brilliant

THERE'S ONLY ONE SURE METHOD OF TURNING DREAMS INTO REALITY ~

IT'S BY A PROCESS CALLED "WAKING UP".

Ashleigh Brilliant

The best reason for having dreams

is that in dreams

no reasons are necessary.

Ashleigh Brilliant

WHEN YOU PLAN
A JOURNEY
FROM
YOUR MIND
INTO MINE,

Ashleigh Brilliant

REMEMBER
TO
ALLOW FOR
THE
TIME
DIFFERENCE.

A TIME WILL COME SOON
WHEN YOU'LL LOSE
ALL CONTROL OF
YOUR BODY
AND MIND...

Ashleigh Brilliant

SLEEP
WELL!

Who's Minding the Body? 67

Pot-Shots BY ASHLEIGH BRILLIANT

© ASHLEIGH BRILLIANT
1985.

NEVER MIND
ABOUT
SHOULD YOU
OR
SHOULDN'T YOU:

THE
QUESTION IS —
WILL YOU
OR
WON'T YOU?

v. Folk Lore

On this occasionally tiresome journey which we all have to make through the world, the engaging spectacle of people being human is still one of the great roadside attractions. Actually, one of our very peculiarities as a species is a tendency to gawk at the peculiar behavior and attitudes of our fellow species-members. Realistic exhibitions of human nature in action — a theater in which we are all professional performers — can usually be relied upon to gather a crowd.

But the show goes on regardless of whether or not anyone is watching or taking notes. Some of the most poignant scenes are never observed, or else they are misunderstood, too little appreciated, soon forgotten. Indeed, that is what makes them so poignant.

Here, then, is a chapter of, for, and about people. But you must bear in mind that it was also written by one of them, which may to some extent diminish its scientific validity. (Interesting as such a work might be from many points of view, we probably would not accept as the last word on the subject a study of dogs written by a dog.)

POT-<u>SHOTS</u> NO. 3175.

Ashleigh
Brilliant

**HERE IS A
GUARANTEED
WAY TO
GET MORE
OF WHAT
YOU WANT:**

**WANT
LESS.**

POT-<u>SHOTS</u> NO. 3203

Many
of the
stories
about
people who
always told
the truth

are lies.

Ashleigh
Brilliant

POT-<u>SHOTS</u> NO. 3233.

Ashleigh
Brilliant

**IT'S
EASY
TO BE
BETTER
THAN
EVERYBODY
ELSE ~**

**WHAT'S HARD
IS GETTING
EVERYBODY
ELSE
TO
ADMIT IT.**

Ashleigh Brilliant

THERE IS NO PAIN
THERE IS NO EVIL
THERE IS NO SENSE
IN SAYING THINGS
LIKE THIS.

Ashleigh Brilliant

THE ONLY REAL PURPOSE OF OUR GROUP IS TO EXCLUDE OTHERS FROM MEMBERSHIP.

POT-SHOTS NO. 3327

IT'S HARD TO DECIDE WHAT TO DO,

BUT I SOLVE IT BY NOT DOING ANYTHING.

© ASHLEIGH BRILLIANT 1985

Ashleigh Brilliant

© ASHLEIGH BRILLIANT 1985.

POT-SHOTS NO. 3231.

Ashleigh Brilliant

NOBODY CAN DO EVERYTHING,

BUT WE CAN NEARLY ALL DO MORE THAN WE THINK WE CAN.

© ASHLEIGH BRILLIANT 1985.

POT-SHOTS NO. 3239.

I BELIEVE

THAT, FOR EVERY WHY,

THERE MUST SOMEWHERE BE A WHY NOT.

Ashleigh Brilliant

POT-SHOTS NO. 3240.
Ashleigh Brilliant

NOBODY MUST EVER KNOW MY TERRIBLE SECRET

WHICH WOULDN'T SEEM SO TERRIBLE IF I COULD TELL SOMEBODY.

POT-SHOTS NO. 3254.
Ashleigh Brilliant

I DON'T MIND HOW HIGH THE STAKES ARE,

SO LONG AS THERE IS ABSOLUTELY

NO RISK.

POT-SHOTS NO. 3291

PEOPLE DON'T ALWAYS KEEP THEIR PROMISES:

THAT'S WHAT MAKES THE PEOPLE WHO DO KEEP THEM SO SPECIAL.

POT-SHOTS NO. 3355.

Ashleigh Brilliant

WHILE TRYING TO DECIDE THE MOST REASONABLE THING TO DO,

PEOPLE SOMETIMES BEHAVE VERY UNREASONABLY.

POT-SHOTS NO. 3219.

Ashleigh Brilliant

SOME PEOPLE CAN'T BE TRUSTED ~

BUT SOME CAN BE TRUSTED MORE THAN YOU THINK THEY CAN.

Ashleigh Brilliant

POT-SHOTS NO. 3220.

HAVE I EVER USED POOR JUDGMENT?

PERHAPS ~ BUT THAT'S SOMETHING OF WHICH I'M STILL

THE FINAL JUDGE.

POT-SHOTS NO. 3403. Ashleigh Brilliant

**APART FROM
THE INEVITABLE,
THE PROBABLE,
AND THE
POSSIBLE,**

THERE'S
VERY LITTLE
I'M
AFRAID
OF.

© ASHLEIGH BRILLIANT 1985.

© ASHLEIGH BRILLIANT 1985   POT-SHOTS NO. 3434.

Why is it
that
time
softens
some people,

and hardens
others?

Ashleigh
Brilliant

POT-SHOTS NO. 3445.

Ashleigh
Brilliant

**SOMETIMES
THE BEST
DEFENSE**

IS A
SKILLFUL
SURRENDER.

© ASHLEIGH BRILLIANT 1985.

Folk Lore 75

POT-SHOTS NO. 3487.

RIGHT NOW

WOULD BE
A GOOD
TIME
TO
POSTPONE
EVERYTHING.

Ashleigh Brilliant

POT-SHOTS NO. 3514.

WHY
DOES IT
SO OFTEN
TAKE A
GENIUS
TO SEE
THE OBVIOUS?

Ashleigh Brilliant

POT-SHOTS NO. 3515.

IN MOST CASES,

ONE WAY
TO INCREASE
YOUR CHANCES OF
GETTING SOMETHING

IS
TO ASK FOR IT.

Ashleigh Brilliant

POT-SHOTS No. 3516.

I DON'T
INSIST ON
TOTAL
HAPPINESS
ALL AT ONCE ~

I'LL AGREE
TO ACCEPT IT
IN REGULAR
INSTALLMENTS.

©ASHLEIGH BRILLIANT 1985.

©ASHLEIGH BRILLIANT 1985.   POT-SHOTS NO. 3253.

YOU
CAN GET
A GREAT
REPUTATION
FOR WISDOM

JUST BY
TELLING PEOPLE
WHAT THEY ALREADY KNOW.

©ASHLEIGH BRILLIANT 1985.   POT-SHOTS NO. 3247.

I'LL NEVER
BELIEVE IT
UNTIL IT'S
SCIENTIFICALLY
PROVEN ~

AND THERE'S NO
SCIENTIFIC PROOF
THAT I'LL
EVER ACCEPT.

Folk Lore 77

GOOD IDEAS ARE COMMON ~ WHAT'S UNCOMMON ARE PEOPLE WHO'LL WORK HARD ENOUGH TO BRING THEM ABOUT.

©ASHLEIGH BRILLIANT 1985.   POT-SHOTS NO. 3471.

POT-SHOTS NO. 3241.

WHAT GOES UP MUST COME DOWN

BUT WHAT COMES DOWN OFTEN WANTS TO GO BACK UP.

©ASHLEIGH BRILLIANT 1985.

©ASHLEIGH BRILLIANT 1985.   POT-SHOTS NO. 3450.

I AM IRREVOCABLY COMMITTED

TO BEING PERMANENTLY INDECISIVE.

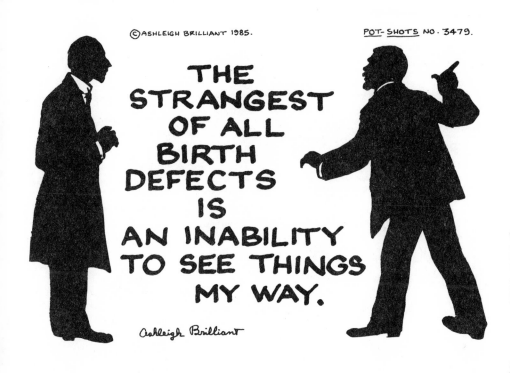

© ASHLEIGH BRILLIANT 1985. POT-SHOTS NO. 3479.

THE STRANGEST OF ALL BIRTH DEFECTS IS AN INABILITY TO SEE THINGS MY WAY.

Ashleigh Brilliant

© ASHLEIGH BRILLIANT 1985 POT-SHOTS NO. 3185

ONE WORLD IS NOT ENOUGH FOR ME

Ashleigh Brilliant

POT-SHOTS NO. 3297.

Ashleigh Brilliant

I CAN'T DECIDE
WITHOUT
FURTHER
INFORMATION,

AND CAN'T
EVEN DECIDE
WHAT FURTHER
INFORMATION
I NEED.

© ASHLEIGH BRILLIANT 1985.

VI. No Business Like the Know Business

We now enter the world of Ideas and Knowledge — a world presided over by a thing called the Brain, which, whatever else you may say about it, is definitely more intelligent than it looks.

The natural history of Ideas is still very much of a mystery. Many have been observed in flight, migrating between the hemispheres of the Brain, but, despite intensive quests motivated by huge rewards, the exact location of their breeding grounds remains unknown. Those which have been captured and dissected seem to contain rich concentrations of a rather common element called Work. But no process of generating Ideas from Work alone has ever yet been developed.

One Idea currently on the wing is that an "Information Revolution" is upon us. Our quest for Knowledge has been so embarrassingly successful that what we most need to find out is what to do with all the things we've been finding out. Facts are accumulating at such an alarming rate that there is now a serious shortage of people to know them.

Science has attempted to come to the rescue by providing us with machines to do our knowing for us. Unlike the Brain, however, those electronic contraptions look more intelligent than they are; and it may yet be some time before they succeed in completely replacing these handy, though much more primitive, knowing-machines, called Books.

MORE BOOKS
HAVE RESULTED
FROM
SOMEBODY'S
NEED TO WRITE
THAN FROM
ANYBODY'S
NEED TO READ.

Ashleigh Brilliant

© ASHLEIGH BRILLIANT 1985.

Ashleigh Brilliant

STAND BACK! ~

I'M GOING
TO
COMMUNICATE.

©ASHLEIGH BRILLIANT 1985.

©ASHLEIGH BRILLIANT 1985.

Self-taught people can be very successful —

BUT ONLY
IF THEY'RE
LUCKY ENOUGH
TO HAVE
EXCELLENT
TEACHERS.

Ashleigh Brilliant

THE INFORMATION
I MOST WANT
IS IN BOOKS
NOT YET WRITTEN

BY PEOPLE
NOT
YET
BORN.

SCIENCE ALONE CANNOT EXPLAIN THE UNIVERSE ~

PLEASE BRING
WHATEVER
HELP YOU CAN
TO YOUR LOCAL
SCIENTIST.

POT-SHOTS NO. 3274.

Ashleigh
Brilliant

I DON'T WANT TO GO HUNTING FOR KNOWLEDGE:

I WANT IT TO COME AND GRAB ME.

POT-SHOTS NO. 3279.

Ashleigh
Brilliant

IT TAKES TIME TO COVER DISTANCE

BUT TIME ALONE ISN'T ENOUGH ~

YOU ALSO NEED SOMETHING CALLED MOVEMENT.

POT-SHOTS NO. 3288.

THERE'S SO MUCH TO LEARN

Ashleigh
Brilliant

AND SO MUCH OF IT NOT WORTH LEARNING.

ISN'T IT WONDERFUL!

INSIDE EVERY
LITTLE BEAM
OF LIGHT,

A RAINBOW
IS SLEEPING.

Ashleigh Brilliant

©ASHLEIGH BRILLIANT 1985

©ASHLEIGH BRILLIANT 1985.

NOBODY HAS YET
DEVISED AN EXPERIMENT
TO SHOW
THE EFFECT ON RATS
OF LIVING MY LIFE.

Ashleigh Brilliant

Ashleigh Brilliant

IT'S EASIER
TO LEARN
MANY
OTHER
THINGS,

IF YOU
FIRST
LEARN
HOW
TO LEARN.

©ASHLEIGH BRILLIANT 1985

No Business Like the Know Business 85

THE PENALTY FOR
NOT KEEPING
IN TOUCH

IS
HAVING LESS
TO FEEL.

© ASHLEIGH BRILLIANT 1985   Ashleigh Brilliant

POT-SHOTS NO. 3286.

READ THIS,
OR
YOU'LL BE SORRY

ON THE
OTHER HAND,
YOU MAY BE
SORRY ANYWAY.

© ASHLEIGH BRILLIANT 1985   Ashleigh Brilliant

POT-SHOTS NO. 3335.

MY WORST
PERSONAL
PROBLEM
IS THAT
MY COMPUTER
DOESN'T
UNDERSTAND ME.

© ASHLEIGH BRILLIANT 1985.   Ashleigh Brilliant

© ASHLEIGH BRILLIANT 1985.   POT-SHOTS NO. 3399.

RELAX!

BETWEEN
THE
INCONCEIVABLY BIG
AND THE
INCONCEIVABLY SMALL,
THERE'S AN AREA
WHERE EVERYTHING
IS
PERFECTLY
CONCEIVABLE!

Ashleigh Brilliant

© ASHLEIGH BRILLIANT 1985.   Ashleigh Brilliant   POT-SHOTS NO. 3318.

IF YOU DON'T WANT TO COMMUNICATE,

FOR GOD'S SAKE
SHUT UP!

POT-SHOTS NO. 3340.

Ashleigh Brilliant

THE TRULY SUCCESSFUL TEACHER

IS THE ONE
YOU WILL
NEVER
NEED
AGAIN.

© ASHLEIGH BRILLIANT 1985.

No Business Like the Know Business

ENORMOUS AMOUNTS OF INFORMATION ARE AVAILABLE,

INCLUDING, HOWEVER, VERY LITTLE RELIABLE DATA ON WHAT IT ALL MEANS.

Ashleigh Brilliant

THE MORE I LEARN ABOUT LIGHT,

THE MORE I THINK WE'RE ALL STILL COMPLETELY IN THE DARK.

Ashleigh Brilliant

CAUTION!

BE VERY CAREFUL OF FALSE, MEANINGLESS, SELF-CONTRADICTORY, AND NOT EVEN VERY FUNNY WARNINGS, LIKE THIS ONE.

POT-SHOTS NO. 3509.

Ashleigh Brilliant

YOU CAN NEVER DISCARD

TOO MANY BAD IDEAS

POT-SHOTS NO. 3402.

DOES IT TAKE MORE ENERGY

TO BE BAD OR TO BE GOOD?

Ashleigh Brilliant

HAVEN'T YOU GOT ANYTHING BETTER TO DO

THAN COMMUNICATE?

I'LL NEVER SAY EVERYTHING THAT'S IN MY MIND,

BECAUSE, FOR MUCH OF IT, NO LANGUAGE YET EXISTS.

THE CLOSEST YOU WILL EVER COME IN THIS LIFE TO AN ORDERLY UNIVERSE IS A GOOD LIBRARY.

No Business Like the Know Business 91

Pot-Shots

BY ASHLEIGH BRILLIANT

POT-SHOTS NO. 3187.

WE COULD HAVE
A MUCH BETTER FUTURE,

IF IT DIDN'T
HAVE TO
BEGIN
WITH
NOW.

Ashleigh
Brilliant

VII. Don't Time Me Down

Sooner or later it seems to occur to even the most amateur thinker that something is going on over which we have appallingly little control, something to which we refer by such lyrical terms as "the process of change" and "the passage of time."

In case you yourself by some chance have not yet become aware of this phenomenon, I challenge you to perform the following experiment: Here and now, try to stop yourself (and everything else) from changing. . . . Not easy, is it? The trick is somehow to condense and isolate your entire existence into the smallest possible fraction of time (or, for best results, into no time at all) — and just stay there.

Those of us lacking the required technique have no choice but to make whatever terms we can with being part of an extremely fidgety Universe, which simply will not keep still, and which insists on eventually changing everything (including us) beyond all recognition.

Of course, this is really only an elaborate game, since, as our common sense tells us, and as Science appears to confirm, you can't turn nothing into something, or vice versa. Whatever is here in this big cosmic mixing bowl, always was here in some form, and presumably always will be. The ingredients simply keep getting rearranged. But I'm sure I speak for many of my fellow ingredients when I say that I wish our own feelings in these matters were taken a little more into consideration.

WHAT
I MOST NEED
AT THIS POINT
IN MY LIFE

*Ashleigh
Brilliant*

IS TO HAVE HAD
A BETTER CHILDHOOD.

*Ashleigh
Brilliant*

YOU'RE ALWAYS
WELCOME TO SHARE
MY MEMORIES ~

TWO CAN
LIVE IN
THE PAST

AS
CHEAPLY
AS ONE.

NO MATTER
HOW LATE IT IS,

*Ashleigh
Brilliant*

IT'S NEVER
AS LATE
AS IT WILL BE,
LATER ON.

POT-SHOTS NO. 3217.
© ASHLEIGH BRILLIANT 1985

DON'T CALL
ANYTHING IMPOSSIBLE,
UNTIL YOU'VE BEEN
ALL THE WAY
THROUGH THE FUTURE.

POT-SHOTS NO. 3260.

TIME MAKES ME UNEASY,
GOING
SO
FAST,

BUT
I'VE FORGOTTEN
THE COMMAND
TO MAKE IT
SLOW DOWN.

© ASHLEIGH BRILLIANT 1985.

POT-SHOTS NO. 3230.

THERE'S
NO
TIME

LIKE
THE
PAST.

© ASHLEIGH BRILLIANT 1985.

ONLY HISTORY CAN DECIDE IF WE WERE RIGHT ~

~ BUT WHAT IF HISTORY CAN'T MAKE UP ITS MIND?

STRANGELY ENOUGH, THIS IS THE PAST THAT SOMEBODY IN THE FUTURE IS LONGING TO GO BACK TO.

Ashleigh Brilliant

YOU CAN SAY GOODBYE TO THE PAST,

BUT YOU CAN NEVER WIPE IT OUT.

© ASHLEIGH BRILLIANT 1985. POT-SHOTS NO. 3486

Ashleigh Brilliant

ALL THIS WILL EVENTUALLY BE FORGOTTEN,

BUT WE WERE REALLY HERE, AND WE KNOW IT REALLY HAPPENED.

© ASHLEIGH BRILLIANT 1985. POT-SHOTS NO. 3342.

FOR SOME REASON, AS TIME PASSES,

I'M EXPECTED TO PLAY THE ROLES OF INCREASINGLY OLDER PEOPLE.

Ashleigh Brilliant

POT-SHOTS NO. 3332.

SAVE HISTORY!

IT'S
THE ONLY
RECORD
WE HAVE
OF
EVERYTHING
THAT'S EVER
HAPPENED.

Ashleigh Brilliant

POT-SHOTS NO. 3405.

DEAD PEOPLE DON'T CHANGE THEIR MINDS,

OR, IF
THEY DO,
IT HASN'T
YET BEEN
WIDELY
PUBLICIZED.

Ashleigh Brilliant

POT-SHOTS NO. 3214.

HOW DID
IT EVER
GET
TO BE
THIS LATE
IN MY
LIFE?

Ashleigh Brilliant

THE BIGGEST PROBLEM ABOUT DEATH
IS HOW TO HANDLE SUCH A LONG PERIOD OF DOING NOTHING.

WE'RE STILL BENEFITING FROM THE SACRIFICES OF PEOPLE LONG DEAD ~

Ashleigh Brilliant

BUT WE'RE ALSO SUFFERING FROM THEIR ERRORS.

Ashleigh Brilliant

IF WE THROW AWAY ALL THE PAST,

WHAT WILL THERE BE TO BUILD THE FUTURE ON?

Don't Time Me Down 99

WHY
DON'T
PEOPLE
GET
BRAVER
AS THEY
GET OLDER?

THE
PAST
HAS ITS
CHARMS,

BUT
NOTHING
NEW
EVER
HAPPENS
THERE.

HOW CAN
IT BE?

AT THE
SAME TIME,
THE PRESENT
IS BECOMING
THE PAST
AND
THE FUTURE.

100

WHAT GOOD IS IT
TO HAVE
LIFE GETTING
BETTER,

IF,
ALL THE TIME,
IT'S GETTING
SHORTER?

AT LEAST,
AS WE GROW OLDER,

WE LOSE
MOST OF
OUR
ABILITY
TO DO
MUCH
HARM.

DEATH
COULD
MAKE
ME

CHANGE
MY
MIND

ABOUT
A LOT
OF
THINGS.

THE MOST EFFECTIVE CURE FOR MIDDLE AGE

IS KNOWN AS OLD AGE.

Ashleigh
Brilliant

Ashleigh
Brilliant

WHY DOES IT ALWAYS GET LATER,

AND NEVER, EVEN ONCE, GET EARLIER?

IF ONLY I COULD GROW,

WITHOUT CHANGING.

Ashleigh
Brilliant

DEATH
IS WHAT HAPPENS WHEN YOUR SUBSCRIPTIONS TO LIFE AND TIME ARE PERMANENTLY DISCONTINUED.

Ashleigh Brilliant

©ASHLEIGH BRILLIANT 1985.

Ashleigh Brilliant

MY ENTIRE LIFE IS BEING RECORDED, FOR PLAY-BACK THROUGHOUT ETERNITY.

©ASHLEIGH BRILLIANT 1985.

POT-SHOTS NO. 3190.

BY THE TIME
YOU
REALIZE
WHAT
LOVE
CAN DO,

THE
DAMAGE
HAS
USUALLY
ALREADY
BEEN
DONE.

Ashleigh
Brilliant

VIII. Close Calls

Try not to be too alarmed if I tell you that not everything and everybody in life can be kept at arm's length. Like it or lump it, close personal relationships with one's fellow passengers on this crowded terrestial spaceship have a way of developing, even though you can never be sure at the outset exactly where they will lead. Sometimes they result in real, abiding friendship — probably one of the most satisfying experiences ever made widely available to the general public. Sometimes they lead to a bewildering event called Progeny. Whatever such encounters produce, however, they invariably make a shambles of your solitude.

But on the other hand, you can't be close to everybody, even if you really would like to be. Considering the statistics, you and I may profess our deep attachment to the Human Family until the cows come home, and still remain perfectly safe from ever being on a first-name basis with the vast majority of the human race, let alone ever having to take it out to dinner, listen to its jokes and complaints, bathe it, or kiss it goodnight.

POT-SHOTS NO. 3193.

Ashleigh
Brilliant

Real love
lasts forever ~

AND,
IN CERTAIN CASES,
THIS CAN BE
VERY
INCONVENIENT.

POT-SHOTS NO. 3338.

MY BEST SOUVENIR
OF ANYWHERE

WOULD BE
A PICTURE
OF YOU
AND ME
THERE
TOGETHER.

Ashleigh
Brilliant

POT-SHOTS NO. 3262.

Ashleigh
Brilliant

WHAT
DOES THIS
MEAN?

~ I'M HAVING FEELINGS
ONLY A PERSON
WHO LOVES YOU
COULD HAVE.

Ashleigh Brilliant

THE ONLY REAL WORLD

IS
THE WORLD
AS SEEN BY
CHILDREN.

MARRYING YOUR OPPONENT
IS SOMETIMES GOOD STRATEGY,

BUT STILL
NO
GUARANTEE
THAT
YOU'LL
EVER
WIN
THE GAME.

Ashleigh Brilliant

NO
MATTER
HOW
HARD
YOU
TRY,

YOU CAN'T
HAVE
GRANDCHILDREN

WITHOUT
FIRST

HAVING
CHILDREN.

Ashleigh Brilliant

IN SOME
UNFORTUNATE
CASES,

THE ONLY WAY
TO EXPRESS LOVE

IS SIMPLY
TO LEAVE
THE PERSON
ALONE.

PLEASE
HELP ME HIDE!

I'M AN
ESCAPED
PRISONER
OF LOVE.

TRAVEL MAKES
THE WORLD
SEEM MORE REAL

BUT
IT CAN
MAKE
HOME
SEEM
LESS
REAL.

JUST BECAUSE I LOVE YOU

DOESN'T NECESSARILY MEAN I FIND IT EASY TO TOLERATE YOU.

Ashleigh Brilliant

Ashleigh Brilliant

MY HAPPINESS DEPENDS SO MUCH ON YOURS

THAT YOU SHOULD FEEL SOME OBLIGATION TO BE HAPPY.

POT-SHOTS NO. 3301.

WHAT VANDAL

CAME
AND
CLEANED
UP
MY ROOM?

POT-SHOTS NO. 3375.

Ashleigh
Brilliant

THERE ARE
SAFER PLACES
THAN HOME,

BUT NONE WHERE
YOU CAN HAVE
SO MANY
STRANGE
ADVENTURES.

POT-SHOTS NO. 3322.

THE BEST WAY
TO HAVE FUN
WITH YOUR
PARENTS

IS
TO TRY
TO PRETEND
THEY'RE
REAL PEOPLE.

What keeps me going
is the thought
that,
somewhere ahead,
is
the next time
I'll see you.

Ashleigh Brilliant

© ASHLEIGH BRILLIANT 1985.

© ASHLEIGH BRILLIANT 1985. POT-<u>SHOTS</u> NO. 3382.

GIVE ME
THE BEDROOM,
BATHROOM,
AND KITCHEN,

AND YOU
CAN HAVE
THE REST
OF
THE HOUSE.

Ashleigh Brilliant

©ASHLEIGH BRILLIANT 1985. POT-<u>SHOTS</u> NO. 3386.

I'm enjoying the story
of our love
so much,

Ashleigh Brilliant

I hope
I never
get to
the end.

SAVE TIME ~

LOVE ME FIRST, GET TO KNOW ME LATER.

Ashleigh Brilliant

WHEN YOU LET ME INTO YOUR HEART,

I had the strangest feeling that I'd been there before.

Ashleigh Brilliant

THINGS LOOK DIFFERENT FROM DIFFERENT ANGLES ~

BUT THERE'S NO ANGLE FROM WHICH I DON'T LOVE YOU.

Ashleigh Brilliant

POT-SHOTS NO. 3454.

I DON'T WANT TO MENTION ANY NAMES,

BUT
THE
PERSON
I LOVE
IS YOU.

Ashleigh Brilliant

 POT-SHOTS NO. 3236.

Ashleigh Brilliant

I CAN READ LIPS ~

BUT
ONLY
WITH
MY OWN.

 POT-SHOTS NO. 3441.

Ashleigh Brilliant

NO MATTER HOW RICH I BECOME,

I'LL NEVER
BE ABLE
TO AFFORD

TO LOSE
YOUR
FRIENDSHIP.

POT-SHOTS NO. 3469.

WHY SHOULD WE GET MARRIED,

AND SPOIL EVERYTHING?

Ashleigh Brilliant

POT-SHOTS NO. 3499.

Ashleigh Brilliant

I NEVER KNEW HOW ALONE IT WAS POSSIBLE TO BE,

UNTIL I FOUND MYSELF WITHOUT YOU.

POT-SHOTS NO. 3481.

LOVE IS THE GREATEST POWER,

Ashleigh Brilliant

BUT NOBODY HAS YET DISCOVERED HOW TO PUT IT INTO A BOMB.

Ashleigh Brilliant

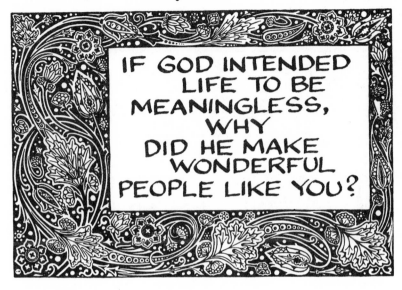

IF GOD INTENDED LIFE TO BE MEANINGLESS, WHY DID HE MAKE WONDERFUL PEOPLE LIKE YOU?

WHEN I CAN NO LONGER LOVE YOU IN ANY WAY WHATSOEVER,

PLEASE CONSIDER ME DEAD.

Ashleigh Brilliant

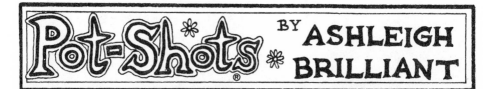

POT-SHOTS NO. 3237.

MY LIFE
SO FAR
HAS BEEN
A LONG
SERIES
OF
THINGS
I WASN'T
READY FOR.

© ASHLEIGH BRILLIANT 1985.

Ashleigh
Brilliant

IX. Life Savor

Time and again, I wake up and find myself undergoing something called Life. Desperately seeking an explanation, a remedy, or at least an apology, all I find, whichever way I turn, is more Life. It seems to go on and on indefinitely, because, by the weird rules of this game, only if you're still actually playing it can you know if the game is over (or know anything else).

There is nothing to compare life with. There is no way of storing it. You can't put a value on it. You can't take it to court. It has no generally agreed-upon purpose. It is totally familiar, and yet incredibly strange. All you can really do with it is BE in it.

So here we are, all of us BEing in life together — and here is somebody like me making little word-and-picture morsels about it for you to partake of, to help sustain you through it. What could be more ordinary, or more extraordinary, than that?

© ASHLEIGH BRILLIANT 1985.

POT-SHOTS NO. 3244.

HERE'S A SIMPLE WAY TO MAKE FEWER CORRECTIONS:

MAKE FEWER MISTAKES.

Ashleigh Brilliant

POT-SHOTS NO. 3222

UNLESS SOME OF MY TROUBLES MOVE OUT,

THERE'LL BE NO ROOM FOR ANY MORE TO MOVE IN.

© ASHLEIGH BRILLIANT 1985

Ashleigh Brilliant

© ASHLEIGH BRILLIANT 1985

POT-SHOTS NO. 3215.

Ashleigh Brilliant

IT'S NO GOOD GOING FAST,

IF ONLY THE SLOWEST PERSON KNOWS THE WAY.

THE EXACT LOCATION OF HELL IS NOT WELL-KNOWN,

EXCEPT
TO THOSE
OF US
WHO'VE
BEEN THERE.

Ashleigh Brilliant

MY DISAPPOINTMENTS COME IN ALL SIZES,

Ashleigh Brilliant

TO
FIT
MY
HOPES.

IF ONLY
SOMEONE
WOULD INVENT
A SOAP
WHICH
COULD
CLEAN
TOMORROW'S
DIRT
TODAY!

Ashleigh Brilliant

Ashleigh Brilliant

LET LIFE BE A LESSON TO YOU!

Ashleigh Brilliant

IS
LIFE
BETTER
UNDERSTOOD

BY LOOKING AT IT
MORE CLOSELY,
OR
BY STEPPING BACK
FARTHER FROM IT?

WHAT ARE USELESS THINGS FOR?

THERE ARE
SO MANY THINGS
I WOULDN'T
HAVE TO DO,

IF I DIDN'T
CARE
ABOUT
STAYING
ALIVE.

SOMETIMES
IT'S TOO MUCH
OF AN
EFFORT
EVEN TO
RETREAT
IN WILD
DISORDER.

MY ROAD'S BEEN MOSTLY UPHILL,

BUT
AT LEAST
THAT MAKES
IT EASIER
IF I WANT
TO STOP.

Ashleigh Brilliant

Ashleigh Brilliant

I WAS HOPING FOR A MIRACLE

BUT
ALL I GOT
WAS
HUMAN
LIFE.

POT-SHOTS NO. 3473.

SOMETHING MUST BE WRONG! ~

I'M ALREADY HAVING REGRETS ABOUT THE FUTURE.

POT-SHOTS NO. 3440.

ONE PROBLEM I HAVE DEFINITELY SOLVED

IS THE PROBLEM OF NOT HAVING ENOUGH TO WORRY ABOUT.

POT-SHOTS NO. 3478.

WHAT'S THE GOOD OF HAVING SOMETHING TO LOOK FORWARD TO,

IF I CAN'T REMEMBER WHAT IT WAS?

REGARDLESS OF THE RISK,

I HAVE DECIDED TO SURVIVE AS LONG AS POSSIBLE.

I REQUIRE NO SPECIAL CONDITIONS FOR MAKING MISTAKES:

I CAN PRODUCE THEM IN PRACTICALLY ANY SITUATION.

SOME PARTS OF MY LIFE SHOULD HAVE BEEN

MORE CAREFULLY EDITED BEFORE THEY WERE RELEASED.

I WISH
TO REPORT
THE
STRANGE
DISAPPEARANCE
OF
MY
HOPES
AND DREAMS.

©ASHLEIGH BRILLIANT 1985.

Ashleigh Brilliant

IT'S NOT EASY
TAKING MY PROBLEMS
ONE AT
A TIME,

POT-<u>SHOTS</u> NO. 3317.

Ashleigh Brilliant

WHEN
THEY
REFUSE
TO GET
IN LINE.

©ASHLEIGH BRILLIANT 1985.

IF YOU HAVE
THE SAME KIND
OF PROBLEMS
I HAVE,

PLEASE SEEK HELP
IMMEDIATELY!

©ASHLEIGH BRILLIANT 1985.

Ashleigh Brilliant

ONE OF THE MOST COMMONLY MADE MISTAKES
IS BEING BORN AT THE WRONG TIME.

Ashleigh Brilliant

LIFE IS OBVIOUSLY A BATTLE,
BUT EXACTLY WHO IS THE ENEMY?

Ashleigh Brilliant

Ashleigh Brilliant

DOING EVERYTHING ON MY LIST
WOULD TAKE STRENGTH,
BUT I HAVEN'T EVEN STRENGTH TO MAKE THE LIST.

No matter what happens, I will always think of myself as being alive.

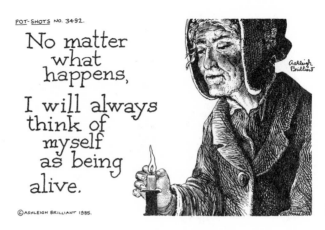

FOR ME, IT WOULD BE VERY UNUSUAL TO HAVE A USUAL DAY.

BY THE TIME I REACH THE END OF MY LIFE, I HOPE I'M READY TO SETTLE DOWN.

POT-SHOTS NO. 3292.

Ashleigh
Brilliant

I'VE HAD
PLENTY OF TIME
TO THINK
SINCE
BEING BORN,

BUT
HAVEN'T YET
REACHED ANY
DEFINITE
CONCLUSION.

x. Think You Very Much

Religion and Philosophy are all very well in their place, and that place, for our present purposes, is none other than this very chapter. Almost anything is fair game for thinkers nowadays, but in the most fashionable contemporary targets, the bullseye will be found to consist of a mere black hole, into which any thoughts that manage to penetrate seem to vanish irretrievably. This creates a continual need for new thoughts, and the Thinking-Industry, a vital component of our national economy, is thereby kept in business.

As a leading manufacturer of processed thoughts, I can report a healthy growth in the demand for many styles of speculation. Accumulated uncertainties, occasioned by dwindling stocks of faith, have led to a sharp increase in shipments of tentative theories, refurbished postulates, and new-model dogmas. The trade continues to be somewhat seasonal, and peak activity on the Thought Exchange usually coincides with slow season in the Accomplishment Industry.

My own share of the market is, of course, limited to those discriminating thought-consumers who prefer small, highly-concentrated packages, with a word-count not exceeding seventeen per unit. This, however, is still sufficient to keep the Brilliant Thoughts® assembly line moving along at full speed, especially now that successful negotiations have put an end to the threat of a strike among suppliers of nouns and verbs.

Ashleigh
Brilliant

**I CAN
ACCEPT
ALMOST
ANYTHING,**

**EXCEPT
WHAT APPEAR
TO BE
THE BASIC
FACTS
OF REALITY.**

© ASHLEIGH BRILLIANT 1985.

POT-SHOTS NO. 3208   © ASHLEIGH BRILLIANT 1985.

**BELIEVING IT
DOESN'T
MAKE IT
TRUE,**

**UNLESS
GOD
ALSO
BELIEVES IT.**

Ashleigh
Brilliant

POT-SHOTS NO. 3490.

**MY
CHURCH
IS
EASILY
CONVERTIBLE**

**TO
WORSHIP
ANY
RESPECTABLE
GOD.**

© ASHLEIGH BRILLIANT 1985.

Ashleigh
Brilliant

130

I know many symbols
for life,
but I don't
yet know
what life
is a symbol
for.

© ASHLEIGH BRILLIANT 1985.

Ashleigh
Brilliant

POT-SHOTS NO. 3331

THE
LINE
MUST
BE
DRAWN
SOME-
WHERE

BUT,
WHEN CIRCUMSTANCES CHANGE,
YOU CAN ALWAYS
DRAW ANOTHER LINE.

© ASHLEIGH BRILLIANT 1985.

Ashleigh
Brilliant

© ASHLEIGH BRILLIANT 1985.

POT-SHOTS NO. 3186.

I KNOW ALL THIS
WILL EVENTUALLY
HAVE
AN END ~

Ashleigh
Brilliant

BUT
WHAT
SHOULD I DO
WITH THAT
KNOWLEDGE?

POT-SHOTS NO. 3213.

SO MANY PEOPLE
WHO TALK
ABOUT
GOD

DON'T KNOW
WHAT
THEY'RE
TALKING
ABOUT.

Ashleigh Brilliant

POT-SHOTS NO. 3421.

THE UNIVERSE IS
MY HOME,

Ashleigh Brilliant

BUT I'M THINKING OF MOVING.

POT-SHOTS NO. 3235.

I WANT TO BE REMEMBERED
AS SOMEBODY
WHO SCORNED THE WHOLE IDEA
OF WANTING TO BE REMEMBERED.

Ashleigh Brilliant

©ASHLEIGH
BRILLIANT
1985.

POT-SHOTS NO. 3267.

THIS WORLD IS
CONVENIENTLY
LOCATED,

ABOUT
HALF-WAY
BETWEEN
HEAVEN AND HELL,

WITH
GOOD VIEWS
IN BOTH
DIRECTIONS.

POT-SHOTS NO. 3400.

WE'RE ALL
PART OF
SOMETHING
WE CAN NEVER
POSSIBLY
UNDERSTAND~

~WHY
DON'T I
FIND THAT
VERY COMFORTING?

©ASHLEIGH
BRILLIANT 1985.

POT-SHOTS NO. 3315.

THERE IS
A GOD!
(BY POPULAR)
DEMAND

©ASHLEIGH BRILLIANT 1985

Think You Very Much 133

THE THINGS I'M PRAYING FOR

SOMETIMES MATTER LESS THAN THE THINGS I'M PRAYING AGAINST.

WE ALL KNOW THAT SOMETHING, SOMEWHERE, IS TRUE BEYOND ALL QUESTION ~

AND WE ARE ALL WRONG.

POT-SHOTS NO. 3391.

THE EXISTENCE
OF GOD

HAS ALREADY
BEEN PROVEN
TO MY
SATISFACTION
BY THE
EXISTENCE
OF
EVERYTHING
ELSE.

POT-SHOTS NO. 3277.

Ashleigh
Brilliant

WHEN YOU'RE
GOING TO HEAVEN,

you always
have
the right of way.

POT-SHOTS NO. 3409.

IN THE FUTURE,
ALL THE SECRETS
OF THE UNIVERSE
WILL EVENTUALLY
BECOME KNOWN:

I CAN
HARDLY
WAIT!

Ashleigh
Brilliant

Think You Very Much 135

POT-SHOTS NO. 3429.

I DON'T KNOW WHAT LIFE IS,

BUT THERE'S ONE THING I'M SURE IT ISN'T:

IT ISN'T EASY.

 POT-SHOTS NO. 3484.

WHERE SHOULD I STAND TO GET THE BEST VIEW OF REALITY?

 POT-SHOTS NO. 3431.

EVENTUALLY, WE ALL HAVE TO TAKE OFF THIS HUMAN COSTUME,

AND PUT ON OUR ETERNITY SUIT.

GREAT POWER IS DANGEROUS WITHOUT GREAT WISDOM ~

AND GREAT WISDOM IS USELESS WITHOUT GREAT POWER.

POT-SHOTS NO. 3296.

©ASHLEIGH BRILLIANT 1985

©ASHLEIGH BRILLIANT 1985.   Ashleigh Brilliant   POT-SHOTS NO. 3456.

ETERNITY MIGHT BE A NICE PLACE TO VISIT, BUT I DON'T THINK I'D WANT TO LIVE THERE.

POT-SHOTS NO. 3433.

GOD'S EXISTENCE WILL BE PROVEN BEYOND ALL DOUBT,

WHEN ENOUGH MONEY IS PUT UP FOR THE PURPOSE.

©ASHLEIGH BRILLIANT 1985.

POT-SHOTS NO. 3483.

IT MUST BE
VERY SAD
TO BE A GOD
NOBODY
BELIEVES IN
ANY MORE.

© ASHLEIGH BRILLIANT 1985.

Ashleigh Brilliant

© ASHLEIGH BRILLIANT 1985.   POT-SHOTS NO. 3470.

Ashleigh Brilliant

I WANT
TO
TAKE HOLD
OF
REALITY~

BUT
SOMEBODY
KEEPS
MOVING IT.

© ASHLEIGH BRILLIANT 1985.   POT-SHOTS NO. 3455.

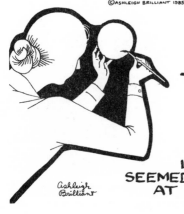

NOBODY
KNOWS
WHY
THE WORLD
WAS
CREATED,

BUT
IT PROBABLY
SEEMED A GOOD IDEA
AT THE TIME.

Ashleigh Brilliant

WHATEVER GOD WANTS,

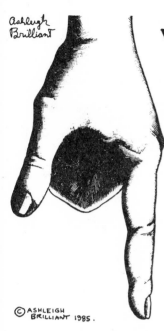

I SECOND THE MOTION.

PARDON MY HASTE ~

I HAVE TO BE OUT OF THE WORLD BY THE END OF MY LIFE.

Pot-Shots *BY* **ASHLEIGH BRILLIANT**

POT-SHOTS NO. 3316.

Ashleigh
Brilliant

WE LIVE IN
A WORLD
WHERE
NOTHING
SEEMS
IMPOSSIBLE

EXCEPT
PEACE
AND
HAPPINESS.

© ASHLEIGH
BRILLIANT 1985.

XI. Thinking the World of You

Every dedicated thinker needs somewhere to think and something to think about — and that may be why we have been provided with a rather unusual place called the World.

It is here in the World that virtually everything of importance (and unimportance) happens. As far as we as people are concerned, this means quite a full schedule of activities, so much so that events frequently overlap, and it can become very hard to separate the often-unruly spectators from the often-unwilling performers. Some kind of management is usually supposed to be in charge, calling itself something like "Law" or "Government," but it generally has trouble even managing itself, and an amusing proclivity for marching onto the field, shattering into opposing fragments, and becoming part of the Show.

Within this crazy arena, Great Affairs and Vital Issues are kicked back and forth so hotly that the goals themselves often have to be shifted and replaced. Nobody has ever been able to decode the scoreboard. Winners are frequently declared before any agreement has been reached as to what game is being played. And it appears that I am not alone in being principally concerned about the location of the refreshment stands.

THIS
WORLD
WOULD BE A NICE PLACE
TO BUILD A CIVILIZATION.

© ASHLEIGH BRILLIANT 1985.

Ashleigh Brilliant

IT MAY BE
THAT

PERPETUAL
PEACE

Ashleigh Brilliant

CAN ONLY
BE
BROUGHT
ABOUT
BY
PERPETUAL
WAR.

© ASHLEIGH BRILLIANT 1985.

Ashleigh
Brilliant

ONE THING
NO LAW CAN
PROTECT YOU
AGAINST

IS
A CHANGE
IN
THE LAW.

©ASHLEIGH BRILLIANT 1985

DO YOU THINK
THERE'S ANY TRUTH
TO THE RUMOR
THAT EVERYTHING
IS
REALLY
O.K.?

Ashleigh
Brilliant

IN HAVING A WAR,

GREAT CARE
MUST BE TAKEN
TO SEE THAT
NOBODY COMES
WHO WASN'T
INVITED.

POT-SHOTS NO.3184

Ashleigh Brilliant

POT-SHOTS NO. 3177.

Ashleigh Brilliant

LET'S PRAY THAT THE PEOPLE IN POWER ARE RIGHT,

BECAUSE,
RIGHT OR WRONG,
THEY HAVE
THE POWER.

Ashleigh Brilliant

POT-SHOTS NO. 3380.

IF WHAT UNITES US MATTERS MORE THAN WHAT DIVIDES US, WHY ARE WE STILL SO DIVIDED?

ISN'T
THERE
SOME WAY
WE CAN SETTLE
OUR DISPUTE,

WITHOUT
RESORTING
TO
AGREEMENT?

Ashleigh Brilliant

Ashleigh Brilliant

IT WOULD
BE NICE
TO COME BACK
TO THE WORLD,

SOMETIME
WHEN IT
ISN'T
SO
CROWDED.

SO MANY
OF US
ARE
PRODUCTS
OF A
BROKEN
WORLD.

Ashleigh Brilliant

Thinking the World of You 145

IF MORE PEOPLE RECEIVED JUSTICE IN THIS WORLD,

THERE'D BE LESS NEED TO BELIEVE IN ANOTHER ONE.

Ashleigh Brilliant

Ashleigh Brilliant

VICTORY OR DEATH!

(IF IT DOESN'T RAIN)

Ashleigh Brilliant

I BELIEVE THERE IS A HIGHER POWER:

IT'S CALLED THE GOVERNMENT.

146

POT-SHOTS NO. 3439.

Ashleigh
Brilliant

ONLY IN
A CRAZY WORLD
WOULD JEWELS
BE WORTH
MORE THAN
TOOLS.

POT-SHOTS NO. 3413.

Ashleigh Brilliant

GENERALLY SPEAKING,
THE VAST MAJORITY
OF PEOPLE
ARE TOTALLY INCAPABLE
OF BEING
GENERALIZED
ABOUT.

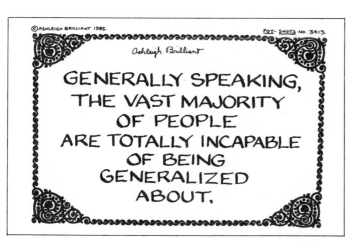

Ashleigh
Brilliant

POT-SHOTS NO. 3290.

THERE IS
NO LAW
AGAINST
DYING ~

COULD THAT BE
ONE OF THE REASONS
WHY PEOPLE STILL DIE?

Ashleigh
Brilliant

NO MORE
REVOLUTIONS, PLEASE~

THIS CENTURY'S QUOTA
IS ALREADY FULL,

AND THERE'S
A LONG
WAITING-
LIST.

Ashleigh
Brilliant

NOTHING
IN THE WORLD
IS BIGGER THAN
A PEOPLE

except a Person.

Ashleigh
Brilliant

THE BIGGER THE CITY
THE MORE
YOU CAN FIND
IN IT

— AND LOSE IN IT.

POT-SHOTS NO. 3226

ONE GOOD THING ABOUT MY COMPUTER:

IT NEVER ASKS WHY.

Ashleigh Brilliant

POT-SHOTS NO. 3497.

Ashleigh Brilliant

WE NEED MORE MONEY FOR DEFENSE ~

TO DEFEND THE GOVERNMENT FROM THE PEOPLE.

POT-SHOTS NO. 3415.

Ashleigh Brilliant

WHAT'S LEGAL ISN'T ALWAYS RIGHT,

AND WHAT'S RIGHT ISN'T ALWAYS LEGAL

~ OR HAVE YOU ALREADY DISCOVERED THAT?

POT- SHOTS NO. 3234.

IN COMMITTING CRIMES
(AS IN MOST OTHER ASPECTS OF LIFE)

IT HELPS
TO HAVE
A GOOD
EDUCATION.

Ashleigh Brilliant

© ASHLEIGH BRILLIANT 1985.

POT- SHOTS NO. 3229.

Ashleigh Brilliant

© ASHLEIGH BRILLIANT 1985

CREATION ALWAYS REQUIRES DESTRUCTION:

BUT
WHAT'S BEING
CREATED
ISN'T ALWAYS
WORTH
WHAT'S BEING
DESTROYED.

POT- SHOTS NO. 3353.

NOT EVEN A
GREAT LEADER
CAN GET
VERY FAR
WITHOUT
GREAT
PEOPLE
TO LEAD.

© ASHLEIGH BRILLIANT 1985.

Ashleigh Brilliant

POT-SHOTS NO. 3299

MANY PAST
WRONGS

CAN
NEVER
BE
RIGHTED,

~ BUT MANY
FUTURE WRONGS
CAN STILL
BE PREVENTED.

Ashleigh Brilliant

POT-SHOTS
NO. 3311.

BEWARE!

FREEDOM
OF SPEECH
ALSO INCLUDES
THE FREEDOM
TO BE
MISUNDERSTOOD.

POT-SHOTS NO. 3179.

IF FORCED TO
CHOOSE,

I'D
ALMOST
ALWAYS
RATHER
EAT
THAN
FIGHT.

Pot-Shots® BY ASHLEIGH BRILLIANT

Ashleigh Brilliant

© ASHLEIGH BRILLIANT 1985.

POT-SHOTS No. 3189.

NO MATTER WHAT ANYBODY SAYS,

we all know
that
having
pleasure
is never
a waste of time.

XII. A Measure of Pleasure

There is no question that you deserve whatever pleasure you can get out of this book, and, since this chapter provides your last chance, I have made at least a nominal effort to assemble in it some choice illuminations from the brighter side of Brilliant.

Never let it be said (except by me) that I don't know how to make people happy. Some of the happiest people in the world are those whom, in one way or another, I have suddenly stopped annoying. If I can't gladden your heart with something you find in these pages, you may at least take comfort from the assurance that no further pitiful efforts will be made herein.

In any case, I hope you'll agree that what really matters is that we have come this far together. We have played our respective roles as writer and reader. Some portion of our minds is forever bonded and sealed in this segment of time. That in itself ought to be a very comforting thought. (But please don't blame me if for some reason it's not!)

SOMETIMES THE GREATEST ACHIEVEMENT OF MY DAY

Ashleigh Brilliant

IS GETTING INTO BED AT NIGHT.

© ASHLEIGH BRILLIANT 1985.

© ASHLEIGH BRILLIANT 1985.

THE MOST EXCITING PLACE TO DISCOVER TALENT

IS IN YOURSELF.

Ashleigh Brilliant

© ASHLEIGH BRILLIANT 1985.

LIFE IS WHAT GOES BY WHILE YOU'RE WATCHING TELEVISION.

Ashleigh Brilliant

I BELIEVE THAT CHOCOLATE IS A FORCE FOR GOOD IN THE WORLD.

© ASHLEIGH BRILLIANT 1985.

Ashleigh Brilliant

A Measure of Pleasure 155

Ashleigh Brilliant

POT-SHOTS NO. 3339.

KEEP LAUGHING AT DEATH,

AND YOU MAY AT LEAST EVENTUALLY DIE LAUGHING.

© ASHLEIGH BRILLIANT 1985.

Ashleigh Brilliant

POT-SHOTS NO. 3365.

TO WHOM SHOULD I APPLY FOR PERMISSION TO BE HUNGRY?

© ASHLEIGH BRILLIANT 1985.

© ASHLEIGH BRILLIANT 1985.

POT-SHOTS NO. 3306.

Ashleigh Brilliant

SHOULD I HURRY TO CATCH UP WITH HAPPINESS,

OR IS HAPPINESS BEHIND ME, HOPING I'LL SLOW DOWN?

DON'T
BE
SURPRISED
IF
SOMEDAY
I SURPRISE
YOU.

Ashleigh Brilliant

Ashleigh Brilliant

IN A WORLD WHERE
EVERYBODY'S
ON THE MOVE,

IT'S A
DISTINCTION
TO
STAY
HAPPILY
IN ONE
PLACE.

GO TO EXTREMES
IF YOU MUST,
BUT
REMEMBER
WHO'S
ALWAYS WAITING
FOR YOU,
BACK IN
THE
MIDDLE.

Ashleigh Brilliant

A Measure of Pleasure 157

POT-SHOTS NO. 3406.

MERRY BAH AND A HAPPY HUMBUG

Ashleigh Brilliant

POT-SHOTS NO. 3464.

TO SETTLE A BET,

WOULD YOU
PLEASE TELL ME
WHETHER OR NOT
THERE REALLY IS
A GOD.

Ashleigh Brilliant

Ashleigh Brilliant

POT-SHOTS NO. 3480.

NOTHING ENDURES LIKE A GOOD SONG,

AND OFTEN,
NOBODY'S
MORE
FORGOTTEN
THAN
THE PERSON
WHO WROTE IT.

IF I WERE DETERMINED TO COMMIT SUICIDE,

I WOULD
FIRST
TRY TO
DO IT
WITH
CHOCOLATE.

I'LL NEVER GET TO HEAVEN,

UNTIL
THERE'S
A
SUBSTANTIAL
REDUCTION
IN THE
FARE.

POT-SHOTS NO. 3224.

WHO NEEDS REAL LIFE?

Ashleigh Brilliant

POT-SHOTS NO. 3428.

Ashleigh Brilliant

YOU CAN'T BUY CHRISTMAS:

YOU HAVE TO MAKE IT.

POT-SHOTS NO. 3394

Ashleigh Brilliant

IN THE GREAT DRAMA OF LIFE,

I'VE BEEN GIVEN THE ROLE OF A LATE-COMER IN THE AUDIENCE.

A UNIVERSE LIKE THIS

COULD ONLY HAVE BEEN CREATED

UNDER THE INFLUENCE OF SOME VERY POWERFUL DRUG.

IF RECORDS ARE MADE TO BE BROKEN,

I JUST HOPE MY BEST ONES ARE BROKEN BY ME.

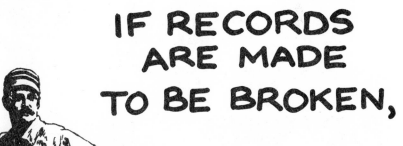

Ashleigh Brilliant

DOING WHAT I WANT TO DO

USUALLY REQUIRES GETTING SOMETHING I HAVEN'T GOT.

Ashleigh Brilliant

IF WE SOLVE ALL THE WORLD'S PROBLEMS AT BREAKFAST,

WE CAN SPEND THE WHOLE DAY HAVING FUN!

Ashleigh Brilliant

UGLINESS CAN BE PRESENT FOR SO LONG, YOU DON'T NOTICE IT ANY MORE ~

BUT SO CAN BEAUTY.

I'm utterly dazzled by your inner beauty

IF LIFE REALLY IS JUST AN ILLUSION,

PLEASE
CONVEY
MY COMPLIMENTS
TO THE
ILLUSIONIST.

Ashleigh Brilliant

NO
MATTER
WHAT
YOUR
RETIREMENT
PLANS,

You can never retire from my life.

Ashleigh Brilliant

Ashleigh
Brilliant

BEING ALIVE SEEMS SO NATURAL TO ME ~

IT'S HARD TO BELIEVE I'LL EVER BE ANYTHING ELSE.

WHAT COULD POSSIBLY BE MORE FANTASTIC

Ashleigh
Brilliant

THAN REALITY?

Let's Keep in Touch

I would have liked to shake your hand — but thank you for at least letting me try to shake your mind. And this isn't really the end, if we don't want it to be. I hope we'll keep running into each other in all the best places, and on all the best products. And if there's a newspaper or other publication where you'd like to meet me regularly, please ask, or if necessary compel, the editor to get in touch with me.

One very pleasant way you can extend our relationship is by sending for my postcard catalogue, which enables you to choose the Brilliant Thoughts® which best meet your personal needs from an amazing variety, including many not found in any store or in any of my books. It comes with sample cards, information about my other books and products, and a splendid order form. The current (1985) price is $2. Please enclose that amount, or its equivalent in your own time and currency.

My address is:

Ashleigh Brilliant
117 W. Valerio Street,
Santa Barbara, California 93101, U.S.A.

Select Bibliography

I. Books and Articles Referring to Ashleigh Brilliant and His Works:

Abraham, Matt. "The T-Shirt Philosopher." *The Advertiser* (Adelaide, Australia), Nov. 28, 1981.

Avery, Pamela. "The 'Brilliants' of a Syndicated Cartoonist." *Rocky Mountain News* (Denver), Feb. 15, 1979.

Berman, Laura. "Some Brilliant Pot-Shots at Life." *Detroit Free Press*, Feb. 8, 1979.

Blum, Walter. "Ashbury's Ash." *San Francisco Examiner*, June 9, 1968.

Boquist, Faye. "Pot-Shots Exude Life's True Ways." *San Jose News*, April 15, 1975.

Bowden, Jane A., ed. *Contemporary Authors*, Vol. 65-68. Detroit: Gale Research Co., 1977, p. 79.

California Magazine. "Brilliant Deduction." Nov. 1984, p. 80.

Carter, Lloyd G. "Author Seeks The Point Of Life." *Los Angeles Times* (from United Press International), Jan. 29, 1984.

Chatfield-Taylor, Joan. "Ashleigh Is Brilliant In 17 Words Or Less." *San Francisco Chronicle*, Oct. 30, 1979.

Conran, Shirley. "Psychological Postcards." *Vanity Fair* (London), March, 1972.

Cool, Margaret. "Those Pithy Pot-Shots." *Santa Barbara Magazine*, Summer, 1980.

Cooper, Candy. "Brilliant Ashleigh Takes Pot-Shots At Himself." *Independent Press-Telegram* (Long Beach, Calif.), July 2, 1980.

Dell, John. "Weak Plot, Ho-Hum Acting Plague Play By Creator of 'Pot-Shots'." *Santa Barbara News-Press*, May 11, 1985.

Denerstein, Robert. "Ashleigh Brilliant: A Billboard For Own Work." *Rocky Mountain News* (Denver), April 25, 1980.

Dewey, Jackie, R.N. "Brilliant Wit and Wisdom: Burnout Antidote." *Health Care Horizons*, (San Pedro, Calif.), March 29, 1981.

Downey, Bill. "Brevity May Be Top Contribution Of Those Brilliant Pot-Shots." *Santa Barbara News-Press*, Nov. 26, 1978.

Godwin, John, Beth Bryant, and Rena Bulkin. *Arthur Frommer's Guide to San Francisco.* New York: Frommer/Pasmontier, 1977, p. 122.

Goldwag, William J., M.D. "A Time For Cheer." *Bestways*, Dec., 1984, p. 10.

Griscom, Elane. "Ashleigh Reviews His Brilliant Career." *Santa Barbara News-Press*, April 25, 1985.

Guernsey, John. "Firing Of Professor Raises Questions: Action Stirs Campus In Bend." *The Sunday Oregonian* (Portland), March 28, 1965.

Gustaitis, Rasa. *Turning On.* New York: Signet, 1969, pp. 200-201.

Helfand, Jerry. "Spicy Pot-Shots Banned In New York." *Santa Barbara News and Review*, July 12, 1979.

Hofstadter, Douglas R.. *Metamagical Themas: Questing for the Essence of Mind and Pattern*, New York: Basic Books, 1985, pp. 47, 732, 803.

Hopper, Ila Grant. "Ashleigh Brilliant Rides Again, Evens Score." *The Bulletin* (Bend, Oregon), Aug. 21, 1976.

Impressions: The Magazine for the Imprinted Sportswear Industry. "The Law: Brilliant Vs. W.B. Productions: Re-defining What Can and Can't Be Copyrighted." Feb. 1980, pp. 146-152.

Jackson, Beverley. "Ashleigh's Cards Brilliant." *Santa Barbara News-Press,* Dec. 9, 1973.

Lillington, Karlin J. "The 17-Words-Or-Less World of Ashleigh Brilliant." *Daily Nexus* (University of California at Santa Barbara), May 23, 1980.

Malan, Andre. "Needled By The Haystacks." *The West Australian* (Perth), Feb. 10, 1973. [Ashleigh Brilliant's one-man protest demonstration against a Perth band's amplified music.]

Mulvihill, Kathleen A. "Witty Words: Great Writing Can Be Brief . . . ." *The Times-Picayune/States Item* (New Orleans), May 25, 1981.

Nelson, Roy Paul. *Cartooning.* Chicago: Henry Regnery, 1975, p. 43.

New Zealand Herald, (Auckland). "New Cartoon Series Begins Today." March 31, 1973.

Orange County Illustrated (Santa Ana, California), "At Palm and Olive." Nov., 1966. [How Ashleigh Brilliant secured a free supply of Palmolive soap for the students of Chapman College's Floating University, whose headquarters happened to be at the corner of PALM and OLIVE Streets in Orange, California.]

Perry, Charles. *The Haight-Ashbury: A History.* New York: Random House, 1984, p. 297.

Phillips, Bill. "Russian Club Achieves Campus Recognition: Brilliant Praises Council Action." *Spartan Daily* (San Jose State College, California), Oct. 23, 1958.

Richmond. "Erstwhile Bournemouth Schoolboy Makes His Fortune In America." *Evening Echo* (Bournemouth, England), May 25, 1971.

Ritter, Carl. "This Group Unified By Diversity." *San Diego Union,* May 30, 1976. [Ashleigh Brilliant and the Mensa Society.]

Scarpinato, Mary, "Hoping to Hit The Target." *St. Louis Globe-Democrat,* April 19, 1975.

Santa Barbara News-Press. "Cartoonist May Sell Patty Note." Oct. 30, 1975. [How a letter from Patty Hearst to Ashleigh Brilliant was offered at auction by the New York autograph firm of Charles Hamilton.]

Santa Barbara News and Review. "Pot-Shots By Crafts Board: Ashleigh's License Axed." Nov. 19, 1976. [Ashleigh Brilliant forbidden to exhibit in local art show because his art contained words.]

Santa Barbara News and Review. "Unpredictable Independents Could Swing City Elections." Feb. 25, 1977. [Running for City Council.]

Sun-Herald (Sydney, Australia). "Scholarly Funny-Man." Jan. 14, 1973.

Thrapp, Dan L. "Postcard Poetry." *Los Angeles Times.* Jan. 12, 1974.

Times-Star (Alameda, Calif.) "Oakland Museum Picks Associate Curator." Sept. 15, 1970.

Upland News (Upland, Calif.) "Likes It Here." Jan. 17, 1957.

Von Hoffman, Nicholas. *We Are the People Our Parents Warned Us Against.* New York: Fawcett, 1968, pp. 10-12.

Who's Who in the West. Chicago: Marquis, 1980 —.

Woman's Day (Australia). "Dr. Brilliant's Tonic." May 20, 1974.

II. Books and Articles in Which (by Special Permission) *Pot Shots®* Are Quoted or Reproduced as Illustrations:

Brown, Mark, and Julius Laffal. *Coping with Mental Disturbance.* Middletown, Ct.: Dept. of Psychology, Connecticut Valley Hospital, 1983.

Cooke, Ann and Frank. *Cooking with Music.* Santa Barbara: Fiesta City Publishers, 1983.

Evans, Terence T., (U.S. District Judge, Eastern District of Wisconsin). "Decision and Order in the Case of *Count Fuller, A/K/A Jeffrey Pergoli v. The Fuller Brush Co.*" Civil Action no. 83-C-592, Oct. 20, 1984.

Giegold, William C. *Management by Objectives.* New York: McGraw-Hill, 1978.

Goleman, Daniel, Trygg Engen, and Anthony Davids. *Introductory Psychology.* New York: Random House, 1982.

Hayward, Susan. *A Guide for the Advanced Soul.* Spit Junction, NSW, Australia: In-Tune Books, 1984.

Heinich, Robert, Michael Molenda, and James D. Russell. *Instructional Media.* New York: John Wiley & Sons, 1982.

Houdart, Francoise. *People.* Paris: Hatier, 1974. [A French text-book series for teaching English.]

Lamb, Charles W. "A Space And A Witness." *Pilgrimage* [Journal of Psychotherapy and Personal Exploration], vol. 11, no. 2, Summer, 1983, pp. 68-78.

Leong, Lim Chong. "My Child Is Smart." *Grow* [magazine for parents and teachers.] Republic of Singapore: Ministry of Education, April 1980.

Reader's Digest. Feb. 1980, p. 242; Sept. 1982, p. 70. In "Quotable Quotes": June 1980 (inside front cover), July 1983, p. 157.

Ryan, Regina Sara, and John W. Travis, M.D. *The Wellness Workbook,* Berkeley: Ten-Speed Press, 1981.

Schaie, K. Warner, and James Geiwitz. *Adult Development and Aging.* Boston: Little, Brown, 1982.

Shapiro, Deane H., Jr. *Precision Nirvana.* Englewood Cliffs, N.J.: Prentice-Hall, 1978.

Short, Robert L. *A Time To Be Born — A Time To Die.* New York: Harper, Row, 1973. [Pot-Shots matched with passages from the Book of Ecclesiastes.]

Swan, Michael. *Kaleidoscope.* Cambridge: Cambridge University Press, 1979. [An anthology of English for non-native speakers.]

Venture Inward [magazine for the Association for Research and Enlightenment], Nov./Dec., 1984.